OBSOLESCENCE IN HOUSING

Obsolescence in housing

Theory and applications

BEV NUTT
BRUCE WALKER
SUSAN HOLLIDAY
DAN SEARS

Joint Unit for Planning Research
University College London

SAXON HOUSE | LEXINGTON BOOKS

Published by

SAXON HOUSE, D. C. Heath Ltd.
Westmead, Farnborough, Hants., England.

Jointly with

LEXINGTON BOOKS, D. C. Heath & Co.
Lexington, Mass. USA.

ISBN 0 347 01105 5
Library of Congress Catalog Card Number 75-31447

Printed in Great Britain by Butler and Tanner, Frome and London

Contents

List of figures

List of tables

Preface

The problem of obsolescence and ageing in buildings has been a continuing theme in the work of the Joint Unit for Planning Research. In 1964 the Ministry of Public Buildings and Works funded a modest study of the patterns of growth and change, of both staff and accommodation, in a number of institutions. These case studies and subsequent research into the office function, demonstrated the importance of obsolescence, but at this early stage no operational method was available with which to extend the research in a rigorous way. However, in 1969, a spin-off from an unrelated area of research enabled us to propose a theoretical framework for future work. As a result, a pilot study of obsolescence in buildings was carried out during 1970. Following this investigation, additional funds were made available in 1972 to support a full-scale study of obsolescence in the housing sector.

The primary aim of this research was to develop techniques for assessing, simulating and alleviating obsolescence in housing. The results of our work are the subject of this book. It is arranged in three parts. The first reviews earlier work in the field and describes a general theoretical framework for examining obsolescence in buildings. In the second part of the book this general theory is applied to the problem of housing obsolescence, and is clarified and developed to the stage of mathematical simulation. Finally in the last part of the book, we describe the results of empirical applications of our approach with some conclusions concerning the management of housing obsolescence in the future.

Many have contributed to the production of this book, our thanks go to all of them. We wish first to acknowledge our sponsors, the Aeronautical and Civil Engineering Committee of the Science Research Council, for the financial support of our research into housing obsolescence. We wish to thank the Human Geography and Planning Committees of the Social Science Research Council for their support of our work in reassessing the residential overcrowding standards and the housing stress index. We wish also to thank the Planning and Transportation Department of the GLC, the Department of the Environment, the South Hampshire Plan Technical Unit and Professor Greve of the University of Southampton for making available to us most of the data on which the study is based. We are also most grateful to the Boroughs of Camden, Enfield and

Richmond, and to Winchester UDC for granting us access to their building regulation files, and to Marketing Advisory Services Ltd, who executed the fieldwork of our adaption survey.

We wish to acknowledge the contribution of Professor Cowan, director of the Joint Unit for Planning Research, whose early research into the problems of growth, change and obsolescence in buildings made our study possible. We wish to thank Ian Cullen for the assistance and advice he has given throughout the project. Finally we wish to thank those who have contributed so much to the support side of the project, especially Lorna Hewitt and Leora Sergay for typing and checking the manuscripts, and those in the computer centre and the duplicating and accounts sections of University College, London.

September 1975   Bev Nutt
                                                     Bruce Walker
                                                     Susan Holliday
                                                     Dan Sears

PART 1

Obsolescence in buildings

1 Introduction

The life histories of buildings are diverse. Between the decisions to construct and destruct lies a varied pattern of existence. Building stock passes through states of occupancy and vacancy, through episodes of use, modification, maintenance, adaptation and extension, until removal by demolition. Buildings differ from most other man-made products; they are place-fixed, they have long physical lives, they entail exceedingly high levels of capital expenditure, and most are in second-hand use. These general characteristics give rise to a number of rather unique life features that affect the onset of obsolescence.

Today's environment is inherited from the past. The location of most of the building stock reflects the economic patterns of the inter-war period and before. Shifts in the location of social and economic activity affect the regional and local demands for building stock. Innovations in transport and communications technology change the relative attractiveness of stock in different areas. The consequences of these factors are accentuated by the long life of buildings. In the developed countries, where permanent rather than temporary buildings are the norm, the life of most buildings is sixty years or more. The potential life of new dwellings is estimated to be in the region of seventy to eighty years.[1] In Britain the annual flow of new buildings rarely amounts to more than 2 per cent of the existing stock. So choice is restricted, in the main, to second-hand stock at locations largely determined by the economic past.

Buildings consume land so the markets in buildings and land are closely related. In Britain private and public ownership exists in parallel, but at present the private sector predominates. Private-sector buildings are particularly vulnerable to speculative forces in the land market. For example, many buildings in central urban areas have been demolished in early or middle life as a result of pressure for more profitable and intensive forms of land development. On the other hand, many public-sector buildings remain underutilised in the absence of effective pressures for greater efficiency. They are protected from market forces, and many continue to support inappropriate functions at uneconomic locations. The high capital cost of buildings and land has led to the emergence of sophisticated credit institutions offering long-term loan facilities. The conditions that these institutions impose have tended to favour conventional forms of design and construction. Moreover, the influence that they exercise is itself subject to political pressures and to short-term financial circumstances in that the rate of investment in new buildings is vulnerable to fluctuations in the money markets and to changes in interest rates.

In most countries, the government regulates the use that is made of buildings. The life histories of buildings are to some extent a function of these regulations and the ways that they have been applied in the past. While the need for some form of regulation is only rarely disputed,[2] legal controls can be slow to respond to changing circumstances. Building and planning regulations tend to freeze the pattern of building into a form that was appropriate to past conditions. The insensitive use of these controls may actually contribute to the current life problems of the building stock and to the onset of obsolescence.[3]

Buildings are initiated in circumstances of high uncertainty about their future lives. However, the act of initiation involves a commitment to physical permanency and spatial fixity. The future uses of buildings cannot be forecast with confidence. At the design and construction stage, the majority of a building's users are unknown. Only the requirements of the first generation of users may be evaluated with any reliability. As a consequence, user requirement studies, market research and user participation are likely to be of short-term value. Most of the building stock designed today will survive to the second half of the next century. Any changes in legislative or individual requirements for building services during this period will have to be accommodated, in the main, within the existing stock. The future likelihood and cost of functional failures in buildings is of considerable concern therefore, to those who are responsible for planning and designing. Here we face a common dilemma. Day to day decisions have to be taken now concerning problems that will only fully emerge in the future. This dilemma is compounded by exogenous changes of an unpredictable kind; changes in physical controls, financial influences and social policies. If we are not to pre-empt the future, we need to investigate the causes and repercussions of partial failures and obsolescence within the planned environment and hopefully produce an early warning system with potential for practical implementation.

Much of the terminology surrounding the study of obsolescence is imprecise. However, most authors do agree that the terms 'obsolete' and 'obsolescence' refer to disuse. The *Oxford Dictionary* defines obsolete as 'disused, discarded or antiquated'. It defines obsolescence as 'becoming obsolete or going out of date'. In the case of most consumer products the term 'obsolescence' refers to the reduction in the usefulness of an object over time. It is commonly agreed that this reduction in usefulness is

4

brought about by the physical deterioration of the product and is hastened by the marketing of newer and better substitutes. So obsolescence is not necessarily equated with deterioration alone, but with the differential deterioration of one object relative to a class of similar objects. For example,

> Where machinery is lessened in value not by mere usage or lapse of time, but by the fact that improved machinery is being brought into use, then this lessened value is termed obsolescence.[4]

> . . . the exhaustion of the usefulness of equipment.[5]

> By definition, when a machine is obsolete there exists an alternative machine or system which is more economical to own and operate.[6]

> Obsolescence is a lessening of use efficiency resulting from the introduction of more desirable systems . . . at the point where a unit does not possess facilities and amenities which society regards as essential for modern living, the accommodation is considered functionally obsolete.[7]

While approaches to the study of obsolescence do vary according to the object under review[8] the basic definitions are reasonably clear. An item of equipment or mode of operation is obsolete when it becomes absolutely useless with respect to a specified function when judged against current standards. Obsolescence, on the other hand, refers to the tendency of objects and operations to 'become obsolete', referring therefore to a process of increasing uselessness. The word 'obsolete' defines the terminal state. Obsolescence describes the transition towards that state.

Defining 'obsolete' and 'obsolescence' in relation to buildings is a far more complex matter. As a result of periodic renovation and reconditioning most items of building stock survive long periods of obsolescence before becoming obsolete. Buildings are only truly defined as obsolete when they have become completely useless with respect to all uses that they might be called upon to support. Demolition usually pre-empts this completely obsolete state. Building obsolescence refers to the degree of 'uselessness' of a building relative to the conditions prevailing in the population of similar building stock as a whole. The relative degree of 'uselessness' will be assessed by the building occupants, the property market, the public, or the planner as the case may be. Obsolescence is therefore a rather subjective and relative term. It usually refers to an opinion made about a particular situation or condition. Such opinions concerning the degree of obsolescence will vary according to the knowledge and viewpoint of the assessor and his awareness of possible alternative states and conditions. The perception of obsolescence also varies in scale from an organisation's view of its own building, to the community's view of local conditions, to the national viewpoint, i.e. to corporate assessments of general building standards and conditions. Collective opinions concerning obsolescence can be gauged therefore, through some statistical account of these perceptions.

The 'degree of uselessness' of a building will vary with time. Actions can be taken to increase the usefulness of buildings and hence reduce their relative obsolescence. Obsolescence should be viewed therefore, as a function of human decision rather than a consequence of 'natural' forces. If no actions are taken then an obsolete state is threatened. The overall likelihood of obsolescence will increase as the service provided by buildings decreases either relative to requirements as demands change, or absolutely as the building stock deteriorates but demands remain constant. So any factor that tends, over time, to reduce the ability or effectiveness of a building to meet the demands of its occupants, relative to other buildings in its class, will contribute towards the obsolescence of that building.

The identification of factors that induce obsolescence has led to a confusingly large number of categorisations. We have physical obsolescence where buildings become increasingly inadequate solely due to the deterioration of their physical fabric.[9] Financial obsolescence has been said to ensue when capital and recurrent expenditure is not balanced by sufficient returns and benefits,[10] bearing in mind that, in the short run, costs usually exceed benefits for a time until the latter are fully realised. Functional and locational obsolescence may develop as building stock becomes unable to support effectively the activities that it contains.[11] Site obsolescence is said to exist when the potential value of a site is high enough to justify redevelopment. Environmental obsolescence of a whole neighbourhood may occur when the conditions in a neighbourhood render it increasingly unfit for its current use.[12] A less clear-cut case is style obsolescence, in which a social group assesses the relative worth of a building or area in terms of its visual and stylistic qualities.[13] Finally, there is control obsolescence where the regulating mechanisms that govern the development and renewal of buildings add to, or even induce, further degrees of obsolescence.[14]

Numerous categorisations of this type have been proposed and discussed. This proliferation has led to considerable confusion in the literature concerning obsolescence. In the following chapter we shall examine and review this work in some detail.

Notes

[1] J.B. Cullingworth in *The Economic Problems of Housing,* A.A. Nevitt (ed.), proceedings of conference held by the International Economics Association, Macmillan, London 1967.

[2] B.H. Siegan, 'The Houston solution: The case for removing public land use controls', *Land-Use Controls Quarterly,* vol. 4, no. 3, summer 1970.

[3] T.L. Blair, 'Twilight-area renewal', *Official Architecture and Planning,* vol. 32, November 1969.

[4] Oxford English Dictionary supplement, 'Obsolescence', quoting W. Hutchinson and F.J.B. Lovell, *Short Dictionary of Legal, Commercial and Economic Terms,* London 1930, p. 87.

[5] K. Lonberg-Holm, 'Time zoning as a preventive of blighted areas', *Architectural Record and Guide,* June 1933, p. 6.

[6] E. Buffa, *Operations Management: Problems and Models,* 2nd. ed., John Wiley, London 1968.

[7] D.A. Kirby, 'The inter-war council dwelling: A study of residential obsolescence and decay', *Town Planning Review,* July 1971, p. 250.

[8] P.C. Cowan, 'Studies in the growth, change and ageing of buildings', *Trans. of the Bartlett Society,* vol. 1, 1962–3.

[9] A.D. Little (Inc.), *Models for Condition Ageing of Residential Structures,* San Francisco Community Renewal Program, Technical Paper no. 2, 1964.

[10] N. Lichfield and Associates, *Economics of Conservation,* York Conservation Study, HMSO, London 1968.

[11] P.C. Cowan, 'Depreciation, ageing and obsolescence', *Architects Journal,* vol. 141, no. 24, June 1965.

[12] D.F. Medhurst and J.P. Lewis, *Urban Decay: An Analysis and Policy,* Macmillan, London 1969.

[13] M. Meyerson, B. Terret and W.L.C. Wheaton, *Housing, People and Cities,* McGraw-Hill, New York 1962.

[14] C. Alexander, *The Coordination of the Urban Rule System,* Working paper no. 1, Centre for Planning and Development Research, University of California, 1966.

2 Concepts of obsolescence

There have been many attempts to explain the causes and repercussions of obsolescence in buildings. Historically they may be divided in three ways. During the early part of this century, obsolescence was viewed mainly as a physical process of deterioration and decay. Physical deterioration with age is the most easily identified form of obsolescence so it is not surprising that this aspect should have dominated early work. The second approach, common during the post-war period, views obsolescence as an essentially economic phenomenon. This approach examines the economic life of buildings, tracing the cycles of investment, depreciation, costs in use and the operational returns. Finally, and recently, the emphasis has shifted towards a behavioural interpretation. A sociological perspective suggests that the built environment reflects the conflicts between those with different power in society,[1] with the stock of 'good quality' and 'obsolescent' buildings helping to perpetuate the existing social structure. Others have adopted a more pragmatic approach. They have examined the typical cycles of change that occur within social organisations as they grow, develop and move from one piece of accommodation to another, and noted when and why certain types of building and location become obsolescent for a particular organisation.[2]

The historic change of emphasis in the study of obsolescence has therefore followed that of planning matters as a whole, shifting from a standpoint of physical, to economic, to social concern. In the discussion that follows, each type of viewpoint will be reviewed in turn. However, these physically based, economically based and behaviourally based views do overlap to a considerable extent and a degree of backtracking and repetition is unavoidable.

The age and condition of buildings

The earliest works to be published this century concerning the physical deterioration of buildings with age, were based on the results of two surveys. The first was a 1917 survey of American railway station buildings.[3] The second was a study carried out in connection with a 1936 survey of the City of London.[4] In the first, the number of

8

renewals to the various parts of the station structure were analysed and depreciation curves produced. The analysis of the second survey showed, that with the exception of a few historic buildings, such as the Guildhall, most buildings in the City experienced some alteration after thirty years, and were abandoned after sixty. The bases and design of this survey are hard to discover, but the conclusions are of interest in view of later estimates of building life.

A more substantial study of changing physical conditions with age, was carried out in connection with a survey of 285 non-rural school buildings in Michigan.[5] An account of the life cycle of these buildings suggested that during the first twenty years some defects did occur, but these were easily corrected. After twenty years, a second phase began. A gradual increase in annual maintenance costs occurred as parts wore out and operating costs accelerated. Many components and much equipment needed to be replaced, but the process of deterioration was not arrested and defects continued to mount after forty or fifty years. Schools then entered a third phase in which functional, site, locational and environmental obsolescence became apparent. Two general conclusions are of interest. First, a distinction was made between 'correctible' obsolescence (e.g. constructional defects and poor services), and 'non-correctible' obsolescence (poor location, inadequate site, unsatisfactory environment). Second, the question of change of use was touched upon and it was concluded that siting had a great bearing on the disposable value of a school.

More recently, much attention has been given to the relationship between age and condition in the housing sector. A number of regression analyses of the 1950 United States census data were undertaken to investigate patterns in the prevalence of substandard housing.[6] The most interesting of these exercises was an attempt to directly correlate poor conditions with age. The results were statistically inconclusive. The direction of association in each case was positive, but there was little difference in the results for each of the age periods used.

An analysis of housing conditions in England and Wales carried out in 1964 indicated an increasing rate of deterioration in the housing stock.[7] Information was gathered from local authorities concerning the number of unfit dwellings by area, together with estimates of the remaining life for fit dwellings. It was concluded that some 3½ per cent of the total national housing stock was unfit, and another 4½ per cent of the total stock had a life expectancy of less than ten years. As a result of the GLC's house condition survey in 1967, some 2½ per cent of London's housing was defined as obsolescent.[8] The concept of obsolescence used in this study was solely that of structural decay and deterioration. It was suggested that the 2½ per cent figure would double by 1975 and more than double again by 1993. This suggestion, that obsolescence in London's housing is rising dramatically, has been queried in a more recent paper,[9] which makes the assumption that no house becomes obsolete within fifty years, but that the probability of a house becoming obsolete thereafter rises by about 10 per cent every decade. When this rather arbitrary assumption was fitted to the age structure in London's housing stock it was found that unless public standards start to rise markedly, the rate at which homes become obsolete is going to increase only slowly during the rest of this century.

The hypothesis, that the physical condition of a building deteriorates with age, is the basis of one of the most important theoretical approaches to the study of obsolescence. In the early sixties an attempt was made to simulate the real-estate market of San Francisco.[10] A 'condition ageing' submodel was used to simulate the physical condition of San Francisco's housing stock at two-yearly intervals.[11] Five categories of physical condition were used in the simulation, ranging from a 'state of good repair' to 'demolished'. The model was based on three Markov matrices whose elements accounted for the probability of transition from one condition state to the next, there being one matrix for each of three defined classes of occupancy. It was implicit in the model that dwellings will only be demolished when they reach an 'unfit' state. However, when the condition-ageing submodel was integrated within the general renewal programme, this assumption was modified so that demolitions resulting from simulated market pressures could also be accounted for.

There appear to be two major criticisms of this condition-ageing model. The model has structural limitations which stem from the scale at which it could be applied. Because of the large volume of data to be handled, it became necessary to employ a very simple mathematical technique and for the number of occupancy classes and condition categories to be severely limited. More seriously, the model depended on a particular theory of physical decay which led to a gross oversimplification of the issue involved. The approach rested on an attempt to adapt a theory of physical decay developed in the physical sciences, to the market for housing. While a fairly sophisticated model of the demand side of the housing market was achieved the supply aspects, especially in relation to the stock of existing buildings, were only crudely treated. It seems probable that, even if some form of decay function could provide an appropriate basis on which to model obsolescence, it would still give a distorted picture of the forces operating on the existing stock of houses.

Deterioration and depreciation

Most of the studies of obsolescence in the immediate post-war period adopted a financial viewpoint. They tried to establish a relationship between the condition of buildings and their market price, linking therefore, the concepts of deterioration and depreciation.

Deterioration has been defined by Ratcliffe as the loss in serviceability and desirability which is the result of physical decay in the components of a building structure.[12] This change in physical condition is reflected in the market price. Depreciation curves can be constructed by graphing the value of the building (excluding land) against its age. The decline in market price, or the loss in liquidation value, is a measure of the amount of depreciation that has occurred over the time period in question. Factors other than physical deterioration must be taken into account. The value of a building is ultimately determined by the demand for its use.[13] Market fluctuations, the timing of purchase and sale, the reduction in the value of money and the deterioration in the environment as a whole, all affect the extent of actual depreciation that results.

The quality of the original structure of a building is an important determinant of the rate of deterioration. So both the rates of deterioration and depreciation can to some extent be controlled by building standards. Ratcliffe suggested that new materials and methods of construction tend to increase the life of buildings and that adequate repair retards depreciation. Furthermore, the rate of obsolescence of mechanical equipment is relatively high compared with that of building structures. With an increasing number of items of mechanical equipment contained in many buildings, the rate of obsolescence is likely to rise in the future. Whether the costs of repair can be justified will depend on market conditions and favourable terms for financing the modernisation and maintenance expenditure.

A number of practical studies of depreciation in the housing sector have been made. The criteria used are crude. For example, an examination of English data from the Midlands provided by professional valuations, found that valuers usually gave houses a life of 100 years with straight-line depreciation.[14] In another paper, the same author discusses some interesting data obtained from the real-estate research programme at Berkeley, California.[15] This data consists of a file of valuations of houses in the Bay area which is kept up to date by a professional valuer. The data include the area of the dwelling, the size of the site and the data of construction. After adjustment of the data to 1962 replacement costs, and accounting for the rises in site value, the analysis data tended to

11

confirm the stated opinions of professional valuers that 'the owner can be relied upon to maintain his house, and that there should be no appreciable physical deterioration or obsolescence for the first twenty years of life'. After that, the hypothesis that it loses 2 per cent of its original value in each succeeding year, and that it becomes valueless at the age of seventy years, appears to fit the data reasonably well.

This is the most convenient and simple description of the process, but it is difficult to explain the nil depreciation during the first twenty years. Other authors take a contrary view. They present graphs of the depreciation in the value of dwellings based on American data and compare these with the increasing value of sites over the same time period.[16] These graphs show an immediate falling off in value of houses from the date of construction.

These apparent contradictions have been at least partially explained in recent years.[17] When dwellings are first built their probable life span is hardly considered by the market, and life expectancy is not specified. In the early years of life there is little or no decline in quality. After the first ten to twenty years, the structure may show minor signs of deterioration or obsolescence. The depreciation curve declines slightly, but may be retarded by the replacement of equipment and remodelling. In this case the owner absorbs the loss due to depreciation. After twenty years, mortgage lenders begin to attach a limited life to the property and to anticipate quality decline even though none may yet be evident. Simultaneously, buyers are reminded of the age of dwelling by restrictive lending policies and this forces the depreciation curve down more steeply. Once decline has begun, a steady downward trend continues. But the rate of decline is diminished in the later stages of life. This is because, on each lower value level, a greater number of families can afford to occupy the structure. Thus there is an increasing pressure against further price reduction. The depreciation curve for most homes therefore flattens, even though deterioration in environmental or physical terms may accelerate, a 10 per cent difference in value representing a greater gap in real quality at the lower end of the scale than the upper.

Thus during the later stages of life, the depreciation curve shows not only physical deterioration, or the sum of money required to restore the unit to some higher level on the value scale, but also the shortage of cheaper dwellings. The expected remaining life of a structure does not diminish further. After fifty years, the market again gives it an unspecified life. Regardless of its age the investors reason that it should last another five or ten years without major reconditioning, and this results in a flattening of the curve. The general conclusion of this explanation is that

12

— assuming the dwelling is not demolished before the end of its economic life and barring the emergence of antique value — the depreciation curve is an inverted S.

Depreciation and taxation

The capital cost of a commercial building is normally written off over a specified number of years by the owner. The write-off period is usually determined for taxation purposes. Logically it should be based on the 'probable life' of the specific class of building involved. Attempts have therefore been made to define probable life and depreciation rates for taxation purposes.

In 1947 the US Department of the Treasury prepared a set of rules concerning the depreciation of property values by assigning a maximum number of years to a building's life. A very loose definition of obsolescence was advanced. 'Obsolescence is the process of becoming obsolete due to progress of the arts and sciences, changed economic conditions, legislation or otherwise, which ultimately results in the retirement or other disposition of the property.'[18] The rules gave a more convincing definition of depreciation and useful life. 'The useful life of buildings depends to a large extent on the suitability of the structure to its use and location, its architectural quality, the rate of change of population, the shifting of land values, as well as the extent of maintenance and rehabilitation.' Depreciation rates were based on the experience of property owners, and allowed for normal obsolescence, or the gradual lessening of useful value. The official depreciation rates did not allow for change in value due to extraordinary events that were unforeseen or unpredictable when the property was acquired.

Some fifteen years after the first publication of the rules, the Department of the Treasury issued a series of revisions.[19] The effect of these was to relax the rules and to give owners more freedom in compiling their allowances. The original and revised rules are summarised in Table 2.1.

In the original rules the equipment within buildings was also given a life span for taxation purposes. In the revised rules the life spans of buildings and equipment were no longer separated. This perhaps partly explains why the revised 'life' guidelines give all building types a shorter life expectancy than in the original rules. Two comments should be made. First, the life of equipment within buildings is consistently shorter than that of buildings themselves. Second, without more knowledge of the precise method of estimating the depreciation rates it is difficult to assess

13

Table 2.1

Estimated building life — US Department of the Treasury

Building type	Estimated life	
	1947	1962–75
Apartments	50	40
Dwellings	60	45
Banks	67	50
Factories	50	45
Garages	60	45
Grain elevators	75	60
Hotels	50	40
Loft buildings	67	50
Machine shops	60	45
Stores	67	50
Office buildings	67	45
Theatres	50	40
Warehouses	75	60

the relative part played by structural or functional factors. Probably the 'general experience of owners' incorporates both factors in varying degrees. Property valuers generally rely on instinct rather than objective measurements in making valuations. One suspects that the same kind of intuition has gone into compiling these rules.

An account of the implications of US taxation practices for the control of urban blight and obsolescence was published in 1950.[20] This suggests that the onset of blight indicates that an area is ripe for more intensive development. In the United States, property taxes are based on the assessed value of the land and buildings. While the value of the land may increase, it is assumed that the value of buildings invariably depreciates with time. As physical conditions deteriorate the cost of public services usually increases. It is suggested that the US tax system tends to exacerbate the problems of urban blight, for as tax revenue declines the cost of urban maintenance goes up.

There is little incentive for an owner to remove obsolete buildings while he can derive a revenue from them. The authors argue that the US and UK property taxes penalise new construction and encourage the retention of old, decayed buildings. Drawing lessons from income-tax methods where the cost of improvements are tax deductible, it has been suggested that, as property deteriorates and contributes to the spread of urban blight, so property taxes should increase. The authors argue that a low tax base for new buildings should be established. During the first ten years the increase in tax would be moderate, after this taxes would gradually accelerate during the ten to thirty-year period. Then tax increases would move rapidly upwards at such a rate that major improvement or complete renewal would be induced at thirty-five years, such improvements returning the building to a lower tax bracket. This approach rejects the traditional assumptions that a building may remain so long as it produces a satisfactory revenue to its owner, and seeks to introduce the idea that a building also provides benefit or disbenefit to the community as a whole.

Another significant interpretation of the phenomenon of obsolescence is that physical deterioration and functional misuse are caused by economic factors. A number of important accounts of obsolescence have resulted, most making use of the notion of costs and benefits. Here the debate has shifted away from the financial issue of depreciation to a broader economic view of the decisions to maintain, to adapt, and to renew. There have been two approaches, the first concentrating on maintenance and adaption expenditure as it arises in individual buildings, the second concerning the problems of urban blight and renewal, and the workings of the land and property market as a whole.

Maintenance and adaption

Obsolescence in an individual building, or in an urban area as a whole, usually entails increasing costs and diminishing benefits over time. In theory a building will become obsolescent when the cost to its present occupier exceeds the benefits of occupation. Stone has described the ways in which the cost of a building may be assessed in terms of its 'cost in use', by combining annual costs with the discounted annual equivalents of capital costs.[21] The evaluation of alternatives involves setting annual equivalent costs against real income, returns or benefits. A major difficulty in rationalising this form of accounting is to distinguish between the operating costs attributable to the building, e.g. maintenance costs and the overall operating costs of the activity which is being carried on in the building. Furthermore, different occupants will have their own subjective sets of values for assessing the returns or benefits of the alternatives open to them. It is often difficult to express all benefits in monetary terms.

The cost—benefit criterion may also be used to interpret decisions concerning change of use. From an economic viewpoint of 'use', a building can be said to be obsolescent in its current use if there is some potential use that promises a greater ratio of benefits over cost. More formally, if a potential use can be found for a building, such that the benefits in that use minus the predicted costs in use and the costs of conversion exceed the benefits in its current use minus current costs in use, then that building is obsolescent in its current use. The current use of the building is therefore defined as obsolescent when

$$X_a - Y_a < X_b - (Y_b + C_{ab})$$

where X_a = current benefit under use a,
$\quad\;\; X_b$ = predicted benefit under use b,
$\quad\;\; Y_a$ = costs in use a per unit time,
$\quad\;\; Y_b$ = predicted costs in use b per unit time
$\quad\;\; C_{ab}$ = conversion costs of change from use a to b, appropriately discounted over the predicted duration of use b.

With similar reasoning, the adaption or renewal of a building is justified economically if the predicted post-change value of the building is greater than the perceived pre-change value plus the estimated cost of effecting the change.[22] So renewal should occur if and only if

$$V_j > (V_i + C_{ij})$$

where V_i = the estimated pre-renewal value of that property at time i,
$\quad\;\; V_j$ = the predicted post-renewal value of the property at time j
$\quad\;\; C_{ij}$ = the predicted capital cost of undertaking the renewal.

This formulation may be applied to the decisions taken by other key agents in the market. Some owners, for example, might decide to sell their building to a property developer should they feel that V_j would be greater than V_i, but find that their current ability to undertake renewal would make C_{ij} so great as to wipe out the predicted increase in value. An established developer, on the other hand, might feel that he would be able to undertake renewal at a sufficiently low C_{ij} to realise a profit.

Kirwan and Martin have defined obsolescence in terms of the lack of maintenance expenditure, adequate to preserve the building in an unchanged physical state.[23] Obsolescence occurs 'when the net benefit that can be derived from undertaking maintenance necessary to keep the condition of a building unchanged or from renewing it, is less than the net benefit of allowing it to continue to be used in its present state or for its present purpose, without any (or adequate) expenditure on maintenance'. This definition has been expressed as follows:

16

$$B_{1A} - (VC_1 + FC_1) < B_{1B} - (VC_1 + FC_1 + MC_1) < B_2 \qquad \text{(i)}$$
$$- (VC_2 + FC_1 + RC_2 + MC_2)$$

$$B_{1A} - (VC_1 + FC_1) > B_{1B} - (VC_1 + FC_1 + MC_1) > B_2 \qquad \text{(ii)}$$
$$- (VC_2 + FC_1 + RC_2 + MC_2)$$

where B = benefit

VC = avoidable costs

FC = unavoidable costs

RC = renewal costs

subscripts $(1, 2)$ = before- and after-renewal expenditure

subscripts (A, B) = without- and with-maintenance expenditure.

In case (i), obsolescence has proceeded to the point at which renewal is the best option; in case (ii), the best option is continued deterioration without maintenance.

Needleman has analysed in depth the decision to rebuild or renovate.[24],[25] He devises a formula to show the maximum cost of modernisation (rehabilitation) compared with the cost of rebuilding (renewal); the relationship takes only economic factors into account. Modernisation is cheaper if

$$b > m + b\,(1+i)^{-\lambda} + \frac{r}{i}\,[1 - (1+i)^{-\lambda}]$$

where b = cost of demolition and rebuilding

m = cost of adequate maintenance

i = rate of interest

λ = useful life of the modernised property

r = the difference in annual repair and rent costs.

This implies that if the cost of renewal is greater than the discounted value of that sum over the life of the modernised property and the difference in repair costs similarly discounted plus an allowance for maintenance, then it is worth modernising that property rather than renewing it. This formula explicitly allows for the opportunity cost of the investment by introducing the interest-rate term i. The difference in annual repair costs, r, is somewhat ambiguous; in the usual case where the repair cost of the modernised dwelling exceeds that for the new dwelling it will presumably be positive. m refers to the maintenance cost of the modernised dwelling. It should be noted that, as mentioned above, Needleman is concerned only with the purely economic aspects of the decision and does not include any allowance for the social costs (such as disturbance) which may be involved.

A number of general conclusions have emerged from theoretical studies of this kind. It has been suggested that the life of an asset depends on the standard of maintenance, and that the lives of many assets can be almost infinitely extended by the replacement of parts.[26] Stone suggests that the optimum amount to spend on maintenance is that which minimises the annual equivalent cost, and: 'Since the annual equivalent of first cost falls so slowly as life is increased beyond 60–70 years, it is not worth much extra annual maintenance cost in order to prolong the life of an asset much beyond this age.'[27] This is because, for most buildings, maintenance costs are small compared with capital service charges, even when the life of the asset is very long. In fact the life of an asset is determined much more by lack of flexibility and high cost of adaptation than by maintenance costs.

A similar view concerning the housing stock has been advanced. Dwellings become unfit for habitation for three reasons: poor quality of construction, wear and tear due to old age and overcrowding, inadequate maintenance.[28] This view suggests that in the rented market the failure of rents to keep up with maintenance expenses has led to rapid deterioration in some dwellings, a few such undesirable buildings causing a whole neighbourhood to become a slum. However, a building's useful life depends on earning power as well as its physical condition. It has been suggested that demolition usually occurs because of changes in demand and that the amortisation of commercial buildings is dependent on the proportion of the income that can be set aside each year rather than on structural life.[29] This view implies that once a building has paid for itself, even if it is structurally sound, there need be no regrets about its demolition. However, if a replacement will not be more 'productive' than the cost of construction and the value of the present building then it is better to improve or rehabilitate.

Urban blight and renewal

Studies of the effects of such factors on urban blight have reached similar conclusions. In an early description, Mumford defines blighted areas as those chronically unable to pay their share of the municipal services essential to their existence, and which are also unable to pay for their own internal renovation and repair. 'The last stage is depopulation: deserted houses, in ruins: no rents: no taxes: a vast economic and civic liability.'[30] A later study defines four kinds of commercial blight: economic, physical, functional and environmental.[31] Economic blight occurs through changes

18

in demand, leading to excessive vacancy rates, or to a lack of specialised services and facilities. The probability of physical blight or deterioration increases with the age and uniformity of an area.

Other authors explain the causes of blight through the combined effects of the independent actions of property owners and speculators.[32] Blight develops when individual owners and planners fail to act. Neither commercial nor public interests will decide to redevelop if the sum of the benefits from renewal would exceed the sum of the costs, social benefits from public facilities being taken into account. Action against blight can be either preventive or reconstructive. It is suggested that the former course involves the co-ordination of decisions on repair and upkeep, whilst the latter course involves intervention by a planning agency.

Another view is that blight can be eliminated simply by renewal, the more difficult problem being to affect the processes that bring it about. Blight, it is argued, is the result of a lack of investment — the economy of an area and the structure of its labour and housing markets having a very important influence.[33] This view has been supported in recent years by those who see blight and decay resulting from the actions of external agents, such as the decisions of urban managers and planners. 'Contrary to popular thought the causes of twilight areas are externally generated forces of change', including the activities of planners.[34] The rather arbitrary decisions made by planners concerning building unfitness due to age are mentioned, together with the vague proposals for redevelopment that can themselves be a principal cause of blight.[35] In the United States it has been argued that government investment in urban renewal may tend to reduce the value of similar property throughout the economy.[36] The notion that taxes on buildings might increase as they get older is again put forward. This would reduce speculative profits being made from decaying buildings. Alternatively, there might be fines for physical deficiencies and incentives for improvement or renewal. Here again we see the idea of controlling blight through the setting of a pre-determined point in time at which a structure should be renewed or demolished.

The filtering concept

A more comprehensive explanation of the process of deterioration and depreciation in the housing sector has been attempted through the theory of filtering. In its broadest sense, filtering describes 'the dynamic aspects of the housing market'.[37] The mechanics of the process are briefly as

19

follows. High-income households are assumed to have a preference for new housing. The market finds it profitable to supply new dwellings to these households, and this supply renders their current dwellings relatively obsolescent for them. High-income households move into the new dwellings creating a surplus of second-hand dwellings which in turn brings about a relative decline in their price. As a result these dwellings are brought within the range of the next-lower income group. Consequently, over time, progressively older dwellings are passed on at lower relative prices to occupants with lower-income levels. At the end of this chain, the oldest housing will be the cheapest, the most obsolescent, and will be occupied by the poorest. The theory suggests that the lowest-income groups benefit indirectly from the provision of dwellings for high-income groups through the handing down of items of stock, and that the faster the rate of new house building for high-income groups the more readily all households can reduce the obsolescence of their current dwellings by moving. With this view, the rate of change of quality for a given price at the bottom of the market becomes a function of the rate of new construction at the top.

There are two distinct elements in this theory: one is the change in occupancy, the other the change in the value of stock. Filtering is defined as 'a change over time in the position of a dwelling unit within the distribution of housing prices as a whole'.[38] This formulation of filtering was broadened in the sixties and explicitly linked with the process of depreciation and obsolescence.[39] It was suggested that style and technological obsolescence started the cycle, deterioration and depreciation kept it going. In this view, filtering occurs if there is a change in the real values of dwelling units over time. Filtering 'up' will cease when the price of an existing unit of given quality equals the supply price of an equivalent new unit. Filtering 'down' will cease when the benefits of occupation no longer cover costs. Here filtering is seen as a valuable process helping to improve housing standards.[40]

The view that the most rapid rate of depreciation takes place during the middle period of a dwelling unit's life was mentioned earlier, there being practically no depreciation at the beginning and end of a building's life. Grigsby has made use of the concept of filtering to provide an explanation for this.[37] At the beginning of the dwelling's life cycle, when it is occupied by people in the upper income bracket, there is a very gradual rate of deterioration and obsolescence. At this time the structure can be easily improved and maintenance is less costly. Towards the end of the dwelling's life when it is occupied by the lower income brackets, the structure is already deteriorated and obsolescent. The slow rate of depreciation here is due to the fact that units which meet only minimum standards are in short supply. But for this shortage the market value of units at minimum standards would fall to a very low level, as with other consumer durables. If technological and style changes were as rapid in the housing market as in the car market, depreciation would — it is suggested — be quickened. The very worst units would be abandoned and there would be even less incentive to spend money on maintenance.

The assumptions on which the theory of filtering is based have been the subject of considerable controversy. The supply of housing is slow to adjust due to its durability, fixed location and the state of the construction industry. The essence of filtering is decline in value but people do not expect to sell their homes at a loss. Thus when a surplus of housing caused by new building which would depress the prices of older structures seems imminent, the market stabilises and the rate of new building falls off.[41] Housing is characterised by many local and other more specialised submarkets, all of which hinder filtering. Some authors see filtering theory as conceptually persuasive but factually inaccurate in that it assumes near-perfect market conditions that are rarely present. They suggest that filtering can only take place in ideal market conditions where there is a small surplus of housing supply over demand for all income groups.[24]

There have been surprisingly few attempts to gain empirical evidence to support such arguments, either for or against the notion of filtering.[42] One investigation studied the change in middle-class housing in thirteen cities in the US, between 1950 and 1960, middle class being defined according to income. It was discovered that the middle class were moving out of the city centre, leaving the upper and lower-income groups behind. This was because of large price/rent differentials between the lower limit for upper-class housing and the upper limit for middle-class housing. It was argued that as a result the upper-class housing did not filter down, thus increasing the pressure for the middle-income groups to migrate from the city. This study found that the greatest change in the middle-class area was due to an expansion of the lower-value housing areas in the city centre. Apart from the city centre, areas of middle-class housing in 1950 were generally middle class in 1960.[43]

It can be concluded that filtering is a limited theory, giving only a partial explanation of the workings of the housing market. Nevertheless the allocation and reallocation processes clearly affects both the rate of improvement or the rate of deterioration, depending on the circumstances. It must therefore have a central place in any theory concerning the process of obsolescence.

Building function and location

Some of the earliest published accounts of obsolescence mention the importance of functional and locational factors. However, with one exception, it is only in recent research that such aspects have received serious consideration. A short paper by Lonberg-Holm, published in the thirties, set out the main factors causing building obsolescence and urban blight.[44] These causes were grouped under four headings:

1 Improvements in design, layout, structural and mechanical equipment; causing obsolescence relative to use.
2 Increasing mobility of population and production, and shifting of functional area; causing obsolescence relative to location.
3 Socio-economic changes, which render obsolete the particular function for which the structure was built.
4 Physical deterioration, caused by wear and tear.

It was suggested that: 'Obsolescence, with the exception of that caused by crowding and physical deterioration is an index of human progress'. Thus the problem is not only to find ways of reducing obsolescence, but also to 'harmonise the growth process through moving or scrapping obsolete equipment'. The concept of 'time zoning' was proposed as a solution to the problems caused by obsolescence. Each building structure would be given a 'parking licence' for a given time on a particular site, with obligation on the erector—owner to renew the structure when the licence expired. Licences would be renewable until occupancy became a public nuisance. This idea was one of the first to connect functional obsolescence with land-use legislation.

A broad functional view of obsolescence has been adopted in most of the work that has been undertaken in the last twenty years. However, attempts to explain the process of obsolescence remain fragmented and diverse. Lichfield, in his study of the economics of conservation in York, lists four aspects of obsolescence: structural, functional, locational and economic.[45] A study of obsolescence in factory buildings in New York suggests inflexibility and environmental degeneration as the major reason for abandoning manufacturing premises.[46] Most authors emphasise the need to understand the forces of growth and change in order to maintain the quality of the environment. The utility of old areas in providing a pool of low-rent accommodation near to the centre of cities is often mentioned.[47] The results of American work suggest that the taste or preference for living in a certain area are based on motives other than those accounted for by economic or spatial theory.[48] It is suggested that the psychological motivations behind the survival of some urban areas, which by all conventional measures could be expected to decline, is a matter needing attention. Most writers seem to agree that functional obsolescence generally precedes structural obsolescence and that much building stock is currently demolished long before it reaches a state of irreversible decay. Blight and obsolescence are seen as inescapable consequences of organisational change and human advance. Most have argued, in a rather general manner, that built-in flexibility and increased investment are necessary if we wish to insure against the early onset of functional obsolescence.

Two approaches need special mention. An important development in the study of obsolescence is summarised by Medhurst and Lewis in their book on urban decay.[49] They note that 'building decay, functional obsolescence and environmental decay are closely interwoven'. They agree with other authors that the actual life of a building depends on the timing and adequacy of maintenance and adaption expenditures, which in turn depend on the adaptability of the original design. Their approach is novel however, in that they view obsolescence as a function of human perception and decision. Their classification is based on the identity of the persons making the assessment of obsolescence. They suggest that tenant obsolescence occurs when the tenant decides that he will gain in total satisfaction by moving out of a given building. Landlord obsolescence occurs when a landlord decides that some step should be taken to alter the condition of the property by improvement or by demolition. The various forces which operate to produce tenant or landlord obsolescence are described. In particular the problem of rental obsolescence is discussed where the current rent for the property becomes inappropriate and needs to be adjusted upwards or downwards. Condition obsolescence occurs when a landlord decides that after taking account of the expenditure involved and the consequent change in expected income, he will benefit by altering the building fabric. Building obsolescence occurs when the building itself is eligible for demolition or reconstruction. The authors point out that building obsolescence arises only after rental or condition obsolescence have been removed, or carefully considered and rejected as being less profitable. Whether one agrees with these categorisations or not, the general premise that the level of obsolescence will depend in part, on the assessor, whether he be landlord, tenant, or owner seems well founded. The incorporation of this subjective aspect into the study of obsolescence is an important step forward.

The second piece of work meriting attention comprises the studies made by Peter Cowan of growth change and ageing in buildings generally,[50],[51] and in hospitals in particular.[52] An early analysis by Cowan included a number of case studies that investigated the relationships between the changing size and functions of organisations and the building that they occupied.[2] The notion of functional obsolescence employed in these studies concerns the relative ability of buildings to support effectively the activities or functions that they contained.

Cowan equates the development of functional obsolescence with the increasing 'misfit' over time between activity requirements and building provisions. This approach has been developed both for the study of individual buildings, and for building-sector stock as a whole. His view of the relationship between activities and buildings and his concept of misfit have provided the foundation for much of the current research into user-requirements and functional obsolescence. He argues that there is a wide variety of building types, some only suitable for a single purpose, others able to accommodate a very wide range of activities. Similarly, some activities can only take place in a particular type of stock, while others can exist in many different types of building. For some activities it is the kind of accommodation that is most crucial, for others locational considerations are paramount. The various items of urban activity can be arranged along a linear scale in which those with highly specialised requirements are placed towards one pole and those with the most generalised requirements are placed towards the other. Here organisations are classified according to the uniqueness of their requirements for buildings and locations. Items of building stock can be arranged in a similar fashion on a 'highly specialised' to 'non-specialised' scale. The multipurpose stock, such as office accommodation and certain types of factory, would be placed at the lower end of this scale. On the other hand, the more specialised building types, such as concert halls, laboratory buildings and hospitals, would cluster towards the upper end.

When these two linear scales are matched, the compatibilities of different types of activity with different types of accommodation are displayed. When the two scales are related through time, the shifting balance between demand and supply is uncovered. This simple model matches only items of activity with items of accommodation and takes no account of the interdependencies linking one type of activity with another, nor of the interrelationships linking elements of the urban fabric. It does not describe therefore, the interface between systems of activity and systems of accommodation. Nevertheless it has provided an important starting point for the study of malfunctioning in the building stock as a whole.

We have seen that the study of obsolescence has been approached in a number of distinct ways. Early work, of a rather rudimentary kind, centred on the process of physical deterioration and led to techniques for modelling condition ageing. Attempts were made to correlate this physical deterioration with rates of depreciation. This rather limited financial approach was developed to assist investment decisions and taxation procedures. In a number of more sophisticated economic studies, the principles of the cost—benefit approach were applied to the problems of obsolescence, as was the general theory of filtering. Recently, increasing interest in the problems of urban decay and obsolescence has led to a proliferation of terms and approaches. The importance of the perception of obsolescence is now recognised, with its associate problems of accounting for preference and choice.

These different notions, concepts and approaches have tended to be partial. The process and consequences of obsolescence in buildings depend on a series of interrelated changes of a social, physical, environmental, economic and political kind that take place at the interface between items of the urban fabric and the organisations that they accommodate. This comprehensive notion of obsolescence is becoming established at a general conceptual level. Despite this however, there are few research methods and operational techniques to help formalise and extend our understanding of obsolescence. There is no integrated theory on which to build.

Notes

[1] J.A. Rex, 'The sociology of a zone of transition' in *Readings in Urban Sociology,* R.E. Pahl (ed.), Pergamon Press, Oxford 1968, p. 215.

[2] P.C. Cowan and A. Sears, *Growth, Change, Adaptability and Location,* mimeo, Joint Unit for Planning Research, London 1966.

[3] ASCE, Committee on Valuation of Public Utilities, 'The life experience of 17 railway stations', *Transactions of the American Society of Constructional Engineers,* vol. lxxxi, December 1917, p. 1557.

[4] City of London, Survey (1936).

[5] R. Winfrey and E.B. Kurtz, *The Life Characteristics of Physical Property,* Iowa State College, 1931.

[6] G.W. Hartman and J.C. Hook, 'Substandard housing in the US: A quantitative analysis' in *Economic Geography,* vol. xxxii, April 1956.

[7] M. Woolf, *Housing Survey in England and Wales,* Government Social Survey, HMSO, London 1967.

[8] GLC Department of Planning and Transportation, *The Condition of London's Housing — A Survey,* Intelligence Unit Research Report, no. 4, 1970.

[9] W.S. Grigson, 'The obsolescence and ageing of London's housing', *GLC Intelligence Unit Quarterly Bulletin,* no. 24, September 1973.

[10] A.D. Little (Inc.), *Simulation Model for Renewal Programming,* San Francisco Community Renewal Program, Technical paper no. 1, 1964.

[11] A.D. Little (Inc.), *Models for Condition Ageing of Residential Structures,* San Francisco Community Renewal Program, Technical paper no. 2, 1964.

[12] R.U. Ratcliffe, *Urban Land Economics,* McGraw-Hill, New York 1949.

[13] M.H. Westhagen, 'A Theory of Obsolescence of Buildings', Ph.D. thesis, Northwestern University, Chicago 1946.

[14] C. Clark, 'Land Taxation' in *Land Values,* P. Hall (ed.), Sweet and Maxwell, London 1965.

[15] C. Clark, 'Values of houses and residential land in the San Francisco Bay area 1940–62', unpublished monograph, 1963.

[16] J. Gottman, *Megalopolis,* Twentieth Century Fund, New York 1961.

[17] W.G. Grigsby, *Housing Markets and Public Policy,* University of Pennsylvania Press, Philadelphia 1963.

[18] US Department of the Treasury, Bulletin F. 1942.

[19] US Department of the Treasury, *Inland Revenue, New Depreciation Rules,* no. 32, July 1962.

[20] A.B. Gallion and S. Eisner, *The Urban Pattern: City Planning and Design,* Van Nostrand, Princeton NJ 1963.

[21] P.A. Stone, *Building Design Evaluation,* Spon, London 1964.

[22] H.B. Fisher, 'Towards the simulation of urban renewal', mimeo, Joint Unit for Planning Research, Seminar paper no. 5, second series, London 1969.

[23] R.M. Kirwan and D.B. Martin, *The Economics of Urban Residential Renewal and Improvement,* Working paper no. 77, Centre for Environmental Studies, London 1972.

[24] L. Needleman, *The Economics of Housing,* Staples Press, London 1965.

[25] L. Needleman, 'The comparative economics of improvement and new building', *Urban Studies,* vol. 6, 1969.

[26] P.A. Stone, 'Housing town development, land and costs', *Estates Gazette,* 1960.

[27] P.A. Stone, 'Economics of Building Designs', *Journal of the Royal Statistical Society,* series A, vol. cxxiii, part 3.

[28] J.P. Lewis, 'British buildings since 1945, and a theory of urban decay', unpublished report to the Royal Institute of British Architects, 1962–3.

[29] J.F.Q. Switzer, 'The life of buildings in an expanding economy', *Chartered Surveyor,* August 1963.

[30] L. Mumford, *The Culture of Cities,* Secker and Warburg, London 1938.

[31] B.J.L. Berry, *Commercial Structure and Commercial Blight,* Research paper, no. 85, Department of Geography, University of Chicago, 1963.

[32] O.A. Davis and C.B. Whinston, 'The economics of urban renewal' in *Urban Renewal,* I.Q. Wilson (ed.), MIT Press, 1966.

[33] L. Wingo, 'Urban renewal: A strategy for information and analysis', *Journal of the American Institute of Planners,* vol. xxxii, no. 3, May 1966.

[34] T.L. Blair, 'Twilight-area renewal', *Official Architecture and Planning,* vol. 32, no. 11, November 1969.

[35] N. Dennis, *People and Planning,* Faber and Faber, London 1970.

[36] J.W. Dyckman and R.R. Isaacs, *Capital Requirements for Urban Development and Renewal,* McGraw-Hill, New York 1961.

[37] W.G. Grigsby, *Housing Markets and Public Policy,* University of Pennsylvania Press, 1963.

[38] R.U. Ratcliff, *Urban Land Economics,* McGraw-Hill, New York 1949.

[39] E.M. Fischer and L. Winnick, 'Reformulation of the filtering concept', *Journal of Social Issues,* vol. vii, nos. I, II, 1962, pp. 47–85.

[40] I. Lowry, 'Filtering and housing standards', *Land Economics,* vol. xxxvi, November 1960, pp. 362–70.

[41] M. Meyerson, B. Jerrett and W.L.C. Wheaton, *Housing, People and Cities,* McGraw-Hill, New York 1962.

[42] See e.g. F.S. Kristof, 'Housing Policy Goals and the Turnover of Housing', *Journal of the American Institute of Planners,* pp. 232–45, August 1965; J.B. Lansing et al., 'New Homes and Poor People: A Study of Chains of Moves', *Ann Arbor Michigan Institute for Social Research,* University of Michigan, 1969; and Centre for Urban and Regional Studies, 'Household Movement in West Central Scotland: A Study of Housing Chains and Filtering', Occasional Paper no. 26, University of Birmingham, 1974.

[43] J.T. Davis, 'Middle class housing in the central city', *Economic Geography,* vol. 41, no. 3, July 1965, pp. 238–51.

[44] K. Lonberg-Holm, 'Time zoning as a preventive of blighted areas', *Architectural Record and Guide,* June 1933, p. 6.

[45] N. Lichfield and Associates, *Economics of Conservation,* York Conservation Study, HMSO, London 1968.

[46] E.M. Hoover and R. Vernon, *Anatomy of a Metropolis: The Changing Distribution of People and Jobs in the New York Metropolitan Region,* Harvard University Press, Cambridge Mass., 1959.

[47] B.J. Frieden, *The Future of Old Neighbourhoods,* MIT Press, Cambridge Mass., 1964.

[48] W. Firey, *Land Use in Boston,* MIT Press, Cambridge Mass., 1947.

[49] D.F. Medhurst and J.P. Lewis, *Urban Decay: An Analysis and Policy,* Macmillan, London 1969.

[50] P.C. Cowan, 'Depreciation, obsolescence and ageing', *Architects Journal,* vol. 141, pp. 1395–1401.

[51] P.C. Cowan, 'Studies in the growth, change and ageing of buildings', *Transactions of the Bartlett Society,* vol. 1, pp. 53–84.

[52] P.C. Cowan and J. Nicholson, 'Growth and change in hospitals', *Transactions of the Bartlett Society,* vol. 3, 1965–6, pp. 63–88.

3   A theory of obsolescence

The various attempts that have been made to interpret obsolescence in physical, economic or functional terms have been discussed. We concluded that each approach is partial and therefore of limited value. Obsolescence in buildings is a phenomenon in which no single facet is always dominant. Any theory about the process of obsolescence in buildings must be capable of accounting for the variety of human actions that may accentuate or alleviate obsolescence and of the mechanics of regulation and control. The theory should integrate these disparate but related factors within a cohesive framework.

General principles

First, we should attempt to clarify the fundamental purpose of a theory of obsolescence. Our concern for the future of the built environment is characterised by two different approaches. We may attempt to describe 'desirable' outcomes for the future. Alternatively, we can try to identify those possible outcomes that would be 'undesirable'. With the first approach, our planning strategies would centre on the attainment with time of desirable goals. With the second approach, our planning will aim to move away from and avoid certain undesirable outcomes. The first approach is positive in character, the second negative. The selection of one approach does not necessarily preclude the other since the two are sometimes complementary.

Before we consider which approach is best suited to the study of obsolescence, we need to look briefly at the issue of 'uncertainty'. It is difficult to estimate the level of uncertainty in a given problem situation. Information theory in general and the notion of 'requisite variety' in particular are useful starting points.[1] However, a simple conceptual view of the issue of 'uncertainty' will be sufficient for our purposes here.

Let us assume that environmental problems have been classified into highly complex, medium and low-complexity issues, the high-uncertainty problem areas being classified as complex, the low-uncertainty problems being classified as low-complexity issues. We may now ask how the fundamental characteristics of problem areas will vary from class to class. Problem areas comprising many variables will cluster in the high-uncertainty class while those with few variables will more frequently give rise to low-uncertainty problems. Long-term and short-term issues will be similarly distributed on our classification frame. Weakly constrained problems will be more common in the high-uncertainty class than those which are tightly constrained. Predominantly qualitative issues will rank higher in uncertainty terms than those of a more quantitative kind. Social problems will be more frequent in the high-uncertainty category than those of a more technical nature. Those planning topics with outcomes that are important to large sectors of the population will generally be found in the high-uncertainty class, while those with outcomes that affect relatively few people will tend to be in the low-uncertainty class.

Exceptions to each of these simple statements can be found, but the broad view does display a familiar pattern. The high-uncertainty area contains the broader planning issues consisting of many variables, lightly constrained and often qualitative, concerning long-term issues with a high social content. On the other hand, the low-uncertainty area is characterised by few variables, predominantly quantitative and tightly constrained, concerning topics of a technical nature over relatively short time cycles. Clearly, the process of obsolescence must be classified as a high-uncertainty issue.

With this in mind we shall return to consider the positive and negative approaches introduced earlier. Comparisons between these approaches tend to revolve around one, crucial question. Are these two types of approaches equally suitable for all the different planning issues that we face? In other words, is the positive goal-oriented approach as suitable in the low-uncertainty problem class as in the high? The same question is addressed to the negative approach.

With low-uncertainty issues a positive goal-orientated approach is usually preferable. The use of the negative approach here can be cumbersome, time consuming and somewhat impracticable. On the other hand, positive approaches to high-uncertainty problems are always, to some degree, suspect. Positive long-term goals are hard to justify. Here negative open-ended approaches are usually safer than Utopian thinking. We would therefore equate the positive approach with low-uncertainty areas and the negative approach with high-uncertainty areas. Naturally it is wiser to adopt a mixed strategy that includes both positive and negative components, but with the accent on either the positive or negative approach depending on the level of uncertainty that is faced. A theory of obsolescence in building should, we believe, provide a primarily negative framework to assist decision taking. It should help to avoid undesirable outcomes of one kind or another and so reduce the probability of early or unnecessary obsolescence in the built environment.

Change and malfunction

Our description of obsolescence in buildings will centre on the process of change that takes place at the interface between building stock and the human organisations it contains and supports.

Each building presents an array of resources to a potential occupier. These resources are of two types: those actually present within the building and those potentially available within the locality. The set of resources offered by one item of building stock and its location will differ from those offered by another. There are qualitative differences in the kind of resources offered and quantitative differences in the amount of resources offered. If we adopt a 'ghost town' approach in which the activities that presently occupy the building stock are ignored, then four major types of resource provision can be identified.

Firstly, there are differences in the physical resources offered by buildings, e.g. in floor area, internal spatial arrangements, age, standards of servicing, structural condition and floor-bearing capacities. Secondly, there are locational differences in the resources offered, e.g. in the sufficiency or scarcity of transport services and the relative availability of skilled manpower, customers or materials. The provision of environmental amenities, shopping and leisure facilities also varies from location to location. Thirdly, buildings differ when they are viewed as a financial resource. Different items of stock imply different costs and returns, and have different rentable, purchase and rateable values. They impose different 'costs in use' as their lives develop. Finally, there are differences in the range of uses which any building might support and in their potential for change and adaptability. There will be a range of possible uses arising out of the physical, locational and financial resource profiles of the stock. However, at any point in time it is likely that only one of these possible uses will be permitted, due to the application of planning controls.

Any item in the array of building stock may therefore be viewed as a package of resources. Each will offer a different combination of resources in terms of its physical, locational, financial and use characteristics. In a similar manner we can compare and contrast the different resource requirements of organisations and their composite activities. We can describe the combinations of resources that are collectively essential for a particular type of activity to take place satisfactorily. Some of the resources required by organisations may be transferred from place to place, others may not. Some are 'mobile', others are 'place-fixed'. The requirements for mobile resources — people, materials, goods, money and information — are those through which an organisation relates to the environment at

31

large. On the other hand, the fixed resources — space, services and plant — are those that primarily involve the building container.

It is through the matching of the resources supplied and the resources demanded that the relative suitability of an organisation's accommodation is assessed. A comparison of an organisation's fixed-resource requirements with the fixed-resource provisions of a range of different buildings will display a number of incompatibilities. First, there may be incompatibilities between the types of resources required and offered. Second, there may be imbalances between the quantities of resource required and offered. A matching process identifies those items of accommodation that do not offer the necessary types or quantities of fixed resource to support the activity in question. If the activity were to locate in one such building then a degree of permanent imbalance would be inevitable. The activity would then have to adapt itself so that its fixed-resource requirements were reduced to the level of the resources available. Similarly, if over time, the fixed-resource requirements of the activity increase and surpass the resources available, the activity must increase its fixed-resource supply by either relocating, extending its premises or establishing subsidiaries at new locations.

A few general observations should be made about the nature of imbalance between activity requirements and building provisions. The physical life spans of buildings are generally far greater than the probable life spans of the human organisations that they support. Activity and community requirements fluctuate rather rapidly. So some time lag between behavioural requirements and physical supply is inevitable. Furthermore, changes that occur within behavioural organisations are often reversible[2] whereas changes to items of building stock are usually irreversible. So changes of an experimental kind that are open to organisations are not usually possible with items of building stock. In the past, steady rates of social change were accommodated through the periodic destruction and renewal of buildings. Rapid social change is now expected, non-change is unusual if not rare. Urban activity is changing at an accelerating rate but the stock of buildings continues to change very slowly as items are restored, removed and replaced. As a result the resources offered by the building stock lags further and further behind the resources demanded by urban activity.

This is not to say that the operation of activities is determined by the pattern of buildings. But an item of building stock, its size, capacity and location do limit the occupant's activities and his freedom to change and develop. Different items of stock exercise different types and degrees of limitation. However, the necessary 'closeness of fit' between human activity and its building container can be very loose indeed. Human activities are tolerant of many different physical situations. Items of space can accommodate a wide variety of activity. Both behavioural tolerance and building adaptability tend to lessen the effects of resource imbalance, acting as cushions to the encroachment of serious malfunctioning.

However if resource imbalances are allowed to intensify with time, then they lead, first to stressful conditions, and ultimately to partial failures of a functional or financial kind. Trends that threaten undesirable outcomes for the future should be understood and controlled now. The symptoms of malfunctioning are often rather obvious and easy to identify but diagnosis of their cause is far more problematic. In urban problems stressful conditions are relative, absolute breakdown is rare. Some areas of potential stress are far more critical to an activity than others, for different cost penalties are associated with different areas and types of failure. The time cycles of failure development are not uniform for all types of organisation and building. Furthermore the operational time cycles of change are such, that for many aspects, a degree of malfunctioning is of slight consequence provided that it persists only for a short time. So in identifying and describing the development of stressful conditions and in estimating the social and economic costs involved, there will rarely be one single diagnostic character that may be cited. The situation is more likely to be one in which multicausation is giving rise to multi-effects. So the onset of malfunctioning and obsolescence will need to be identified through a whole series of symptoms that may be complexly interrelated one with another. More particularly, we must account for those combinations of change that lead, over time, to increasing degrees of resource imbalance, focusing on the interface conditions that give rise to disutility, disbenefit and dissatisfaction. The description must operate at different levels of aggregation. It should encompass the set of relations between the resources offered and the resources required at at least three levels: the national and regional situation, the conditions of the local urban area, and in the circumstances of particular organisations occupying individual buildings.

The process of obsolescence

The use of a simple notation will assist the description. Let $[B]$ denote a behavioural system, that is, a collection of interrelated items of activity. $[B]$ is defined by some vector $b_1, b_2, b_3, \ldots$ of measurable attributes of the system. It may include the number, duration and frequency of the activities comprising the system: it will describe the character of relations between activities and the number and type of people involved. Similarly, let $[P]$ denote a physical system which can be described as the built container for $[B]$. $[P]$ will define a vector p_1, p_2, p_3, ... of measurable characteristics of the building, its size, condition, spatial arrangement, the services and environmental standards that it provides.

In describing the process of obsolescence, we shall be concerned with the changing relationship between these two vectors. There will be some attributes of $[P]$ which have little effect on $[B]$. Conversely, some attributes of $[B]$ will have no direct effect on $[P]$. We shall be primarily concerned here with the components of $[P]$ and $[B]$ which interact directly.

We have suggested that obsolescence is a relative term referring to the degree of uselessness of some item of building stock — relative, that is, to other buildings in its class. The degree of uselessness will depend on the mismatch between the physical provisions of $[P]$ and the behavioural requirements of $[B]$. More formally, if $[F]$ represents the array of potential mismatches or partial failures between a behaviour organisation and its building container, then

$$[F] = f([P],[B]) \qquad (3.1)$$

Between the time (t) and $(t+1)$ a drift towards increasing mismatch will have occurred when

$$[F]_{(t+1)} > [F]_t \qquad (3.2)$$

The building will become obsolescent for the particular organisation only when $[F]$ reaches an upper level of unacceptability, a level at which no actions are considered feasible to modify either the provisions afforded by the building or the requirements of the organisation, such that the inequality in (3.2) is reversed. More precisely, if the collection of resources offered by a building are denoted by a vector $[R_P]$ of provisions, and if the resources demanded by an organisation are denoted by a vector $[R_B]$ of operational requirements, then a building will be satisfactory as far as fixed resources are concerned provided that $[R_P] \geqslant [R_B]$. Should this inequality be reversed, then a situation of stress or partial failure will have developed. This may be rectified without the activity relocating if activity or building adaptions are possible that serve to reverse the inequality so that balance is restored. When account is taken for the tolerance between organisations and buildings, then in resource terms, imbalance will increase and obsolescence is threatened when:

$$| (R_B \cdot T_B) - (R_P \cdot T_P) |_{(t+1)} > | (R_B \cdot T_B) - (R_P \cdot T_P) |_{(t)} \qquad (3.3)$$

34

where T_B and T_P represent behavioural tolerance of the organisation $[B]$ and the adaptability potential of the building $[P]$ respectively.

This is an oversimplified view. The contributions that the environment at large may make to resource imbalance, and hence to the onset of obsolescence, have been ignored. The vector $[R]$ represents the set of resources r_1, r_2, r_3 ... identified in some system B of organisations B_1, B_2 ... B_n. If a lack of resources is not to lead to serious imbalance and partial failure in some organisation B_i in this system, then

$$I_i - O_i \geqslant Q_i - Y_i \qquad (3.4)$$

and to avoid resource saturation and wastage:

$$I_i - O_i \leqslant X_i - Y_i \qquad (3.5)$$

where I_i, O_i — inputs and outputs of mobile resources to and from B_i per unit time,

Y_i — resources contained in B_i at any point in time,

X_i — resource absorption or storage capacity of B_i in building P_i

Q_i — minimum amounts of resource required, both for inputs and outputs per unit time, necessary for B_i to function satisfactorily.

The term X_i needs some explanation. The fixed-resource provisions of building $[P]_i$ impose capacity constraints on the mobile resources that may be contained, e.g. floor area (a fixed resource), sets an upper limit to the number of people (a mobile resource) that may engage in B_i at that spatial address. Generally, if capacity limitations are not to induce failures then

$$Q_i \leqslant X_i \qquad (3.6)$$

We can put system totals to each of the terms listed above through summations of the usual form

$$Y_N = \sum_{i=1}^{n} Y_i \qquad (3.7)$$

We can also write down a series of input–output expressions:

$$I_i = \sum_{j=1}^{n} Y_{ji} + Y_{Ei}; \quad O_i = \sum_{j=1}^{n} Y_{ij} + Y_{iE} \qquad (3.8)$$

where Y_{Ei} and Y_{iE} are the inputs and outputs between B_i and organisations outside the system under investigation. If I_B and O_B denote the resource inputs and outputs to and from the system as a whole then we

35

have similar boundary values as in expressions (3.4) and (3.5) for resource lack and saturation at system level.

$$I_B - O_B \geqslant Q_N - Y_N \qquad (3.9)$$

$$I_B - O_B \leqslant X_N - Y_N \qquad (3.10)$$

where $I_B = \sum\limits_{i=1}^{n} Y_{Ei}$ and $O_B = \sum\limits_{i=1}^{n} Y_{iE}$

Now, of the total resource output O_N from each of the organisations comprising the system, some resource $(O_N - O_B)$ will remain within the system. Similarly, the total resource input I_N to all activities in the system will be made up of two components, the resource from within the system and that from without. So we may include the usual 'conservation of energy' type statements:

$$(O_N - O_B) \geqslant (I_N - I_B); \quad O_i \leqslant Y_i + I_i; \quad O_B \leqslant Y_N + I_B \qquad (3.11)$$

This description is similar to the traditional form of resource input–output accounting[3] and is summarised in Figure 3.1.

Theoretical formulations of this kind take no account of the various actions that may be taken to control input and output values; they do not describe the ways in which the resource system can be regulated. While resource imbalances are important, we would argue that legislative, social and economic controls also markedly affect the development of obsolescence. Our theoretical description should take account of the limitations, of one kind or another, that are imposed by items of building stock on building occupiers. It should also account for the multiple actions taken by organisations to modify or change the resources provided by the buildings that they occupy. Instead of evolving positive indices or performance standards concerning building use, we are suggesting a 'negative' approach that assesses the package of constraints that various situations impose on different organisations. The approach also assesses the variety of actions that may be taken in response to such constraints. In this way we can account for both sides of the potential conflict between the factors inducing obsolescence on the one hand, and the areas of possible alleviation on the other. They are described through two interrelated notions, the notion of constraint and the notion of response.

The notion of constraint

From a mathematical viewpoint, anything that restricts the number of variables or the values that variables may take is a constraint. Constraint is

36

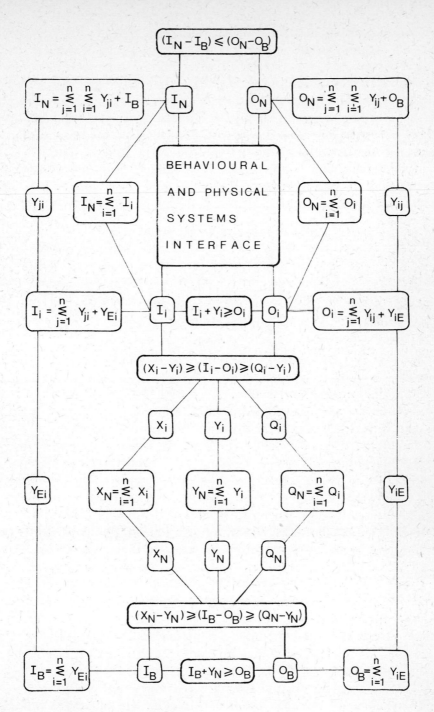

Figure 3.1   Resource formulation

37

therefore a relation between two sets and occurs when the variety that exists under one condition is less than the variety under another.[1] So by definition, constraint is a comparative concept involving at least two different states or conditions. When these states are separated in time, a dynamic approach is possible in which the relative degrees of constraint indicate whether tightening or freeing tendencies are occurring. While this notion of constraint is well established and has been employed in innumerable mathematical applications, the more general notion of constraint has not found common use in social and environmental areas of investigation. It is not however a completely novel approach in these areas. For example,

> Certainly one of the advantages of the emphasis on constraints rather than choice, is that it is possible to get objective indices of the constraints and measure the effect on activity or consumption patterns . . . . I think we should concern ourselves with understanding the constraints and let the choices look after themselves.[4]

And

> Some authors believe that the study of negative determinants might be the safest kind of social science.[5]

The notion of constraint enables us to encompass all of the major facets of obsolescence within a common frame of reference. For example, we can identify spatial constraints, the limitations imposed on an organisation by a building's size and its address. There are facility and condition constraints that affect the uses a building can support. There are financial constraints concerning the consequences of occupation or ownership when expressed in money terms and tenural constraints concerning the legal conditions of use. There are a variety of locational constraints imposed by land-use patterns, the transportation infrastructure and by the physical and social environment of an area as a whole. There are market constraints limiting the ease with which organisations may move through the stock to improve the conditions of their accommodation. Finally, there are legislative constraints that apply to the use and management of buildings through time.

This notion of constraint may be applied at differing levels of aggregation. At the micro level, it may be employed in investigations of the life patterns of individuals through space and time.[6] At the macro scale, it is of equal value. Poverty, congestion, environmental pollution, housing stress, planning blight and resource starvation are all debilitating constraints to human well-being. In this respect many activities aimed at

38

improving welfare are actions to relax the tight constraints that surround the most underprivileged in any society.

Furthermore a comparison of the types and degrees of constraint, before and after some action has been taken, permits the evaluation of the 'constraint relaxation' achieved. This measure provides a way of assessing the disutility or disbenefit that has been removed by the action or response. The degrees of constraint relaxation achieved by alternative strategies may be compared directly with the alternative costs involved, as in a traditional cost–benefit approach.

The notion of constraint therefore provides a comprehensive way in which the wide variety of factors that may induce or reduce obsolescence can be incorporated within one conceptual framework. If the degree of building obsolescence is increasing then this process can be described and measured by the tightening, over time, of the set of constraints imposed on organisations by their accommodation. If the degree of building obsolescence is decreasing then it can be described and measured by the rate of constraint relaxation being achieved.

Now the system of constraints imposed on a behavioural organisation or individual may, or may not, elicit some response from that organisation or individual to modify the current constraint profile. To understand such responses, we would have to examine the ways in which the constraints are actually perceived. Critical questions occur. Are the present and potential occupiers of building stock seeking the best accommodation to support their activities, or merely 'good' accommodation? Is an optimal or a satisfactory level of functional performance required?

We believe that the central task here is to distinguish between the conditions that are just satisfactory and those that are unsatisfactory. This is a distinction between acceptable and unacceptable degrees of constraint imposed by the built environment on any organisation. If we are able to define the range of satisfactory values, covering all facets of obsolescence shown to be important, then a circumstance that meets all these values may be judged to be reasonably good. In time, and with general improvements, standards concerning 'satisfactory' conditions will become more exacting. In order to establish such standards, we wish to know at which point the physical attributes of a building constrain the behavioural attributes of the occupying organisation so that unacceptable levels of stress are occurring. Similarly, at the larger scale, we wish to know at what point the attributes of the physical environment constrain the attributes of the social environment so that intolerable conditions are experienced. How should we begin to interpret the process of obsolescence in 'constraint' terms? At the micro level, we wish to be able to evaluate the

39

constraints imposed by single buildings on individual organisations. At the macro level, we wish to be able to evaluate any debilitating constraints imposed by the built environment over the social environment as a whole. In both circumstances, we wish to be able to take a dynamic view and monitor the changes in these constraints over time, examining whether tightening or relaxing tendencies are occurring.

Basic formulation

We shall consider the case of a single item of built stock with a single occupying organisation although the reasoning applies at both the micro and macro scale. Let the vector of physical attributes of the stock be $[P]_1$ and $[P]_2$ at times t_1 and t_2 respectively. In a similar way, let $[B]_1$ and $[B]_2$ represent behavioural system attributes at t_1 and t_2. If we assume that external conditions in the social and physical environment remain constant during the period t_1 to t_2, then the changing set of constraints which occur at the activity–accommodation interface, within this the simplest dynamic view, are represented by C_{11}, C_{22}, C_{12} and C_{21} in Figure 3.2.

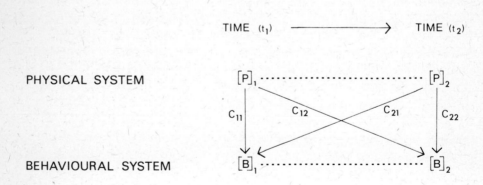

Figure 3.2   A schematic view of constraints through time

Here C_{11} is the vector of initial constraint at time t_1 imposed by $[P]_1$ on $[B]_1$. C_{22} represents the degree of constraint at time t_2 imposed by $[P]_2$ on $[B]_2$. The remaining sets of constraints, C_{12} and C_{21}, will sometimes be hypothetical but they are most important to our line of reasoning. Constraint C_{12} is that imposed by $[P]_1$ on $[B]_2$; it is the constraint arising after some change in the behavioural organisation has occurred, but

40

with no corresponding change to the physical building stock. Constraint C_{21} is that imposed by a changed building $[P]_2$ on an unchanged organisation $[B]_1$. If we compare these sets of constraint, taken two at a time, some useful principles emerge. All six possibilities are examined.

(i)   The comparison of C_{11} with C_{12} describes the difference in the levels of constraint before and after some reorganisation in $[B]$ has taken place. Generally if $[B]$ grows or develops between t_1 and t_2 then it will be more tightly constrained at t_2 than at t_1 and $C_{12} > C_{11}$. The converse will normally apply if $[B]$ is 'running down'. This need not always be the case however. Rationalisation and automation exercises to $[B]_1$ may actually reduce the degree of constraint to $[B]_2$. Hence the direction of the inequality in this relation will signify whether the level of constraint imposed by an item of building stock $[P]$ is increasing or decreasing, i.e. whether the likelihood of obsolescence is becoming greater or is diminishing from the individual viewpoint of the organisation $[B]$.

(ii)   The comparison of C_{11} with C_{21} describes the difference in the levels of constraint before and after some change to the building $[P]$. C_{11} minus C_{21} gives a measure of the potential benefit, whether negative or positive, resulting from the change to the physical system. It accounts for the different set of resources offered by the changed $[P]$ and indicates the potential amount of constraint relaxation achieved by the change from $[P]_1$ to $[P]_2$.

(iii)   The comparison of C_{11} and C_{22} describes the actual benefit derived from the change after the organisation $[B]_1$ that occupied the original $[P]_1$ has itself changed to $[B]_2$ in order to utilise the new set of conditions available in $[P]_2$. The value of C_{11} minus C_{22} will indicate the 'realised' constraint relaxation between the situations at times t_1 and t_2 once stable conditions have returned after both behavioural and physical change. Such benefits, measured negatively through the amount of constraint relaxation achieved, may be related to the monetary costs of alternative physical changes as in traditional cost–benefit analysis. The difference between the results of the comparisons of C_{11} with C_{21} and C_{11} with C_{22}, the difference between the potential and actual benefits, is an indicator of $[B]$'s efficiency in realising the advantages of the physical change.

(iv)   The set of constraints C_{21} are normally the least tight of the four sets illustrated in Figure 3.2, provided that the change $[P]_1$ to $[P]_2$ is not in any way a contraction of the physical system. On the other hand, C_{12} will generally be the tightest constraint of the four. Thus C_{12} and C_{21} might be expected to set the boundary values to the region of constraint in which we are interested during the time period in question.

(v)   The comparison of C_{12} with C_{22} may appear to be of general interest only. The comparison is most important however for planning purposes. At time t_1, given an expected or desired future state $[B]_2$ of the behavioural system at t_2 and an acceptable level of constraint C_{22}, then C_{12} minus C_{22} gives an estimate of the constraint relaxation that will be required. This in turn helps during planning, to specify the necessary form of $[P]_2$ for the required constraint relaxation to be achieved.

(vi)   The comparison of C_{21} with C_{22} is rather hypothetical. C_{22} minus C_{21} indicates the 'realised benefit' to $[B]$. It is a measure of the constraint relaxation achieved and is particularly relevant as a framework for considering the benefits of moving from one building to another.

With this broad theoretical framework we can begin to consider constraint over time, and the ways in which the constraints may be modified by human intervention.

Constraint and response

From a practical viewpoint, the physical changes to items of building stock are in the main overt and can be readily identified and recorded. From a theoretical viewpoint, the 'step-function' transformations that occur in buildings are easier to measure and handle than the continuous and more subtle changes that occur within social organisations. Physical improvements in buildings only occur when an organisation has taken active and expensive steps to effect the change. It is reasonable to expect that changes of this kind are not lightly undertaken; they are major responses to important or serious deficiencies. Seven types of action are possible in the case of individual buildings:

1   Internal adaptions
2   Expansion or contraction of the occupied building stock at the same location by undertaking or terminating subletting, or by the physical expansion of the building.
3   Expansion or contraction of the total amount of stock in use by acquiring additional sites or relinquishing existing sites.
4   Rehabilitation or major conversion.
5   Demolition of an existing building followed by redevelopment at the same location.
6   Relocation to a different building at a new address.
7   Change in the controls affecting building stock — changes in tenure, changes of permitted use, and so on.

42

Behavioural changes within organisations are less easily identified. They may be experimental or innovational in nature and not necessarily reflect an underlying deficiency in the *status quo*. The costs incurred are rarely of the same magnitude as those connected with physical change. General socio-economic changes and those of an institutional kind are even more problematical. Identification is difficult, due both to the relatively long time spans involved and the gradual nature of most changes at high levels of aggregation. Three important classes of behavioural change may however be identified:

1   Changes to the component activities within an organisation – the birth, death, or modification of types of activity.
2   Quantitative changes to populations, activity durations and activity frequencies within an organisation.
3   Structural changes within an organisation – reorganisations, rationalisations and development changes.

These physical and behavioural changes frequently occur together. Within each organisation there is some decision making unit that perceives the states of the physical and behavioural systems and predicts the likely degrees of constraint for some limited time in the future period. As a result of these predictions a set of strategies of response will be considered in order to maintain or relax current constraint levels. A summary list of the more critical change situations and response strategies are given in Tables 3.1 and 3.2. The alternatives listed are not comprehensive but cover the most common circumstances. The types of constraint that are listed have been divided into primary and secondary categories. Primary constraints include the quantities of the behavioural and economic resources within an organisation. An imbalance in one, or a combination of resource requirements and resource availability, will lead to a situation of stress within that organisation which may, unless some controlling strategy is available, lead to partial failures within the behavioural system. Secondary constraints concern those physical back-up resources that are on offer within items of building stock. It is these secondary constraints that themselves constrain the types, quantities, and arrangement of the 'primary' resources within the social organisation in question. Our main concern in studying obsolescence is to model the contributions, both positive and negative, that secondary constraints are making to the primary constraints.

We can measure each type of constraint listed in Table 3.2. A degree of partial failure will be threatened when the constraints are judged to be 'unacceptable' to a significant proportion of current or would-be occupants. If the drift towards obsolescence is to be reversed, action must be

43

Table 3.1

Primary constraints

Constraint	Potential failures	Possible response
Amount of activity within $[B]$ measured in people/hours	< amount of people/hours minimally required by $[B]$	increase population within $[B]$ and/or activity duration reduce requirement
	> amount of people/hours required by $[B]$	converse of above
Amount of goods and materials within $[B]$	< amounts required by $[B]$	increase storage capacity, supply, or lines of supply reduce requirement by rationalisation, etc.
	> amounts required by $[B]$	converse of above
Amounts of information and skills within $[B]$	< amounts required by $[B]$	recruitment and/or improving lines of communication reduce requirement
	> amounts required by $[B]$	rationalise information flows, etc.
Financial resources within $[B]$	< financial resources minimally required by $[B]$	increase resources decrease requirement
Output of resources from $[B]$ per unit time	< output required (i.e. minimum performance standard)	increase output by rationalisation, automation, improved sales, contacts, etc. decrease minimum requirement by raising cost of produced item, reducing overheads, etc.
Resources inputs to $[B]$ from $[E_B]$ per unit time (resources of people, goods, information, cash, etc.)	< inputs required by $[B]$ to sustain adequate functioning	increase inputs, modifying the types of linkage between $[B]$ and $[E_B]$, increase efficiency of transfer, relocation, etc. increase inputs by promoting the transfer of resources from $[E_B]$ to underprivileged $[B]$ reduce requirements
	> inputs that may possibly be absorbed by $[B]$	converse of above
The number, type and positions of communication channels linking $[P]$ with $[E_P]$	< channels minimally required by $[B]$ to communicate with $[E_B]$	change requirement of $[B]$ by use of alternative modes of communication relocate $[B]$ action by agencies in $[E_B]$ to change channels in $[E_P]$
Spare capacity of channels linking $[P]$ with $[E_P]$ by hour	< $[B]$ requirements for transmitting resources to and from $[E_B]$	as above plus modified timetabling of supply and distribution
Cost of channel usage	> cost required by $[B]$ for satisfactory financial position	reduce cost by rationalising communication, or by moving increase income by raised prices, etc.

Key
$[B]$ Behavioural system
$[P]$ Physical system
$[E_B]$ Behavioural environment
$[E_P]$ Physical environment

Table 3.2

Secondary constraints

Constraint	Potential failure	Possible response
Total floor area in [P] by type of resource profile	< total area required by [B]	reduce requirement by lowering space/person, increasing utilisation, reducing population, rationalising space wastage, changing activities, etc. increase provision
	> total area required by [B]	reduce provision by subletting, etc. increase requirement by expansion, etc.
Number of spaces in [P] by type of resources offered (facilities)	< numbers of spaces required by [B]	reduce requirement by lowering privacy standards, intensifying timetable, reducing population, and activity durations, etc. increase provision by internal adaptions
Area (room) size distributions in [P] by type of resources offered	≠ size distribution required	change requirement by modifying group sizes and work routines, etc. change distribution of space
Spatial connectivity of elements within [P]	≠ spatial connectivity required	reorganise requirement modify spatial organisation
Duration of tenure of [P]	< duration required by [B]	modify requirement by contingency plans, etc. renegotiate terms plan move
Cost of space in [P] per year (either rent or amortisation plus maintenance, rates, etc.)	> cost required by [B] for satisfactory financial position	reduce cost by subletting space, restricting maintenance, moving, etc. increase income
Total floor area of built stock in $[E_P]$ by type of resource profile (facilities) offered per sector	< total area required by type to support $[E_B]$ (including vacancy rate)	reduce requirement of $[E_B]$ by reducing population, changing land usage, reducing standards, etc. increase area available by increasing density (i.e. floor space index)
	> total area required	converse of above
Numbers of items of built stock in $[E_P]$ by type, sizes, and tenure	≠ number, type, size, and tenure of stock required to support $[E_B]$	adjust demand structure through planning controls adjust distribution of stock by adaption, rehabilitation, redevelopment, change of use, etc.
Connectivity of building elements within $[E_P]$ and to outside world	≠ connectivity required for $[E_B]$ to operate satisfactorily	modify transportation routes within $[E_P]$
Capacities of the communication networks within $[E_P]$	< requirements for transferring resources to and fro within $[E_B]$	traffic management long term planning action to reduce amount of generated traffic action to modify, change or increase channel provision

Key
[B]   Behavioural system
[P]   Physical system
$[E_B]$ Behavioural environment
$[E_P]$ Physical environment

taken to reduce the degree of constraint to 'acceptable' or 'tolerable' levels. These areas of constraint, the failures that they threaten and the responses they can induce, provide the basis for modelling the process of obsolescence. We shall conclude this theoretical discussion of obsolescence with an outline specification for model building.

A general specification for model building

We may now take an integrative view of the topics that have been discussed and hence specify the general theoretical framework necessary to model obsolescence. Such a model must account for both the areas of threatened obsolescence on the one hand and the areas of possible alleviating action on the other. Our approach rests therefore, on the coupling of the systems of failure and the systems of control. The primary focus of our model-building effort is addressed to those variables that form the bridgehead between the areas of potential constraint and the areas of possible response. We need to explore the ways in which individual areas of constraint are interrelated so that a mathematical description of systems of potential failure is achieved. We need to examine the strategies, both existing and possible, to relax each type of constraint and so model the systems of possible response. Through this dual view of constraint and response it is possible to devise a general diagnostic model with which to simulate the process of obsolescence and to examine systematically the effectiveness of different response strategies in combating obsolescence. The format for such a model is shown in Figure 3.3.

The changing relationships between physical and behavioural attributes are identified in the first stage of the model. The variables that make up the activity–accommodation system under investigation are p_1, p_2, p_3 . . . of physical attributes and b_1, b_2, b_3 . . . of behavioural attributes. The physical attributes are generally regarded as constant in any given situation unless modifying actions are taken. The behavioural attributes of organisations are normally regarded as variable. The possible developments in this system may be simulated by inducing changes in the $[P] \times [B]$ matrix. These changes will be of two general types — quantitative and structural. With quantitative change some measure concerning a system element or relationship varies over time. With structural change the existing pattern of system elements, their interrelationship and operational rules are modified, or new patterns are created, by the introduction, adaption or removal of elements and links within the system, or by parameter changes.

46

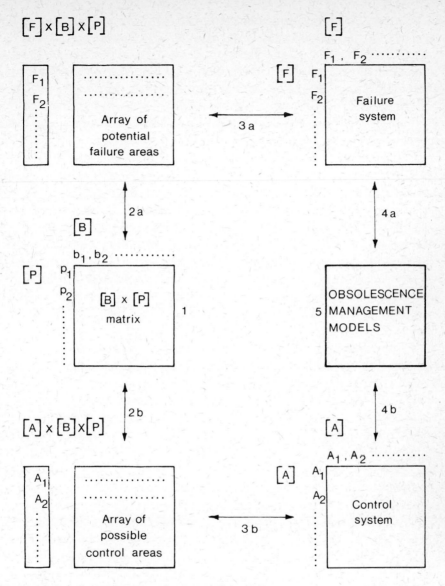

Figure 3.3   Specification for model building

Key   [B]   Set of behavioural attributes of organisations
      [P]   Set of physical attributes of buildings
      [F]   Set of potential areas of failure with 'unacceptable' levels of
            constraint
      [A]   Set of possible response strategies to achieve 'acceptable' levels
            of constraint

We are only concerned with a small part of this picture, i.e. with those possible changes that would threaten partial failure in the system. The use of a systems approach to model building raises a number of well-known problems. In order to give a true picture of an urban system the elements in [P] and [B] must, of necessity, be very numerous. On the other hand if this picture is to have practical value for studying the possible 'futures' of the system then the elements must be restricted to a very small number indeed. In system-theory terms, we need to preserve in our description a good deal of the huge 'variety' inherent in the real-life phenomenon otherwise the characteristics in which we are interested will grossly oversimplify. But the high 'variety' in our description will itself, in turn, prohibit a rigorous study of system development. Logically we need to examine the extremely large system, logistically we need to keep the system small. Our negative approach and the notion of constraint resolves much of this dilemma. For once we redirect our attention to look only at those aspects of the system that might lead to a degree of failure then a systems approach becomes more feasible.

The areas of potential failure deriving from the areas of mismatch are examined through a series of simple equations of the form

$$F_j = f(P_j, B_j) \tag{3.12}$$

where P_j and B_j are subsets of P and B respectively, that contribute to F_j – the area of mismatch in question. This is shown as stage 2a in Figure 3.3. The total collection of potential failures of this sort is displayed in the array [F]. The areas of possible response or control are examined in a similar way in the array [A] (stage 2b) by means of expressions of the form

$$A_i = f(P_i, B_i) \tag{3.13}$$

Severe constraint in one area often exaggerates the level of constraint in others, partial failure in one area often triggers off failure in another. Any area of failure F_j will be potentially related to F_i if they both contain a common variable. Similarly, any two types of response or control will potentially interact if they involve at least one common variable. A systematic view of areas of potential failure and areas of possible response is therefore gained in stages 3a and b, by an examination of the [F] × [F] and the [A] × [A] matrices. Here the issues of failure and responses are linked together through the shared variables in [P] and [B]. This dual view – areas of potential failure and areas of possible response – is the basis for modelling the decision processes from which 'change' or 'no change' states occur at the activity–accommodation interface.

The generality of the broad specification summarised in Figure 3.3 enables us to see how a number of specific submodels might be co-ordinated.

The independent transformations of certain classes of [B] can be simulated in order to identify the points at which they reach states where the constraints imposed by the physical system reach the critical thresholds at which conditions are judged to be unacceptable. For each [B] state there will be some statistical distribution of degrees of constraint imposed by [P], ranging from 'no perceived constraint', to 'intolerable' and 'unacceptable'. An economic submodel could relate the cost penalties of such states to the costs of the alternative response strategies available. The benefits accruing from these strategies would be evaluated in terms of the constraint relaxation achieved. We should stress that the use of constraints and constraint relaxation links the issues of functional failure and response strategies in a very direct way and decision submodels can be developed to link states of [B] and [P] at various levels of aggregation.

Finally, a general simulation model can be developed with which to examine alternative forms of failure developments. Starting from a stable position, where no partial or general failures are occurring and given the existing controls, disturbances can be induced into the model and the repercussions of partial failures simulated for the system as a whole. Controls, economic and behavioural assumptions (e.g. levels of activity, resource requirements and constraint thresholds) can also be manipulated in order to plot the consequent lines of development. So by focusing on two critical aspects of obsolescence — areas of constraint, areas of response — and modelling them, we are able to examine and describe the possible courses of obsolescence for single items of building stock and for urban areas as a whole, and warn of trends that need watching.[7]

Notes

[1] W.R. Ashby, *An Introduction to Cybernetics,* Chapman and Hall, London 1956.

[2] P.C. Cowan, 'On irreversibility', *Architectural Design,* September 1969.

[3] A.G. Wilson, *The Integration of Accounting and Location Theory Frameworks in Urban Modelling,* Working paper no. 11, Centre for Environmental Studies, London 1968.

[4] R.E. Pahl, *Spatial Structure and Social Structure,* Working paper no. 10, Centre for Environmental Studies, London 1968.

[5] T. Hagerstrand, 'What about people' in *Regional Science Association, Papers,* vol. xxiv, 1970.

[6] I.G. Cullen, 'Space, time, and the disruption of behaviour in cities', *Environment and Planning,* vol. 4, 1972, pp. 459–70.

[7] Some of the material included in this chapter was first published in *Environment and Planning*, vol. 4, 1972 and in *Architectural Design*, vol. 40, 1970.

PART 2

Housing obsolescence

4 The process of obsolescence

A theoretical framework for describing and explaining the process of obsolescence in buildings has been outlined. We have suggested that the severity of obsolescence in a particular building is dependent on its relative usefulness when assessed against the prevailing conditions in the class of stock as a whole. In the housing sector the term 'obsolescence' will therefore refer to the relative degree of uselessness or disutility as assessed by the occupants themselves, or by the landlord, the property market or the planner, as the case may be. The perception of obsolescence will vary in scale from the individual's view of his own housing conditions to the local community's awareness of poor housing areas, to the national viewpoint, i.e. to a socio-political view of general housing standards and conditions. We have suggested that the degree of obsolescence can be gauged through those characteristics of the housing environment that constrain their occupants. We originally hypothesised that certain characteristics of dwellings and their environment would constrain households, giving rise to various degrees of dissatisfaction. Furthermore, it was anticipated that these constraining factors would provide a practical way in which the relative severity of dissatisfaction could be gauged. We expected that a comparison of the types and degrees of housing constraint, before and after some remedial action had been taken, would produce a direct measure of the constraint relaxation achieved. Our study of housing obsolescence has therefore examined the changes that take place over time, in the set of housing constraints. More particularly, it has concentrated on those changes that lead, over time, to increasing degrees of imbalance between demand and supply, focusing on those circumstances that give rise to high levels of disutility, disbenefit and dissatisfaction.

The nature of housing obsolescence

Politicians and planners seem to agree that in recent years a slight national surplus of housing stock over households has been achieved. Severe imbalances between the distribution of dwellings and households persist. The problems imposed by imbalance between the housing resources offered and housing resources required are well recognised. Limited employment

53

opportunities induce high levels of migration from some areas. A considerable surplus of old housing stock usually results. This contributes to the typical picture of decline — a reducing local tax base, cut-backs in community services, a depressed housing market, low levels of maintenance, fabric deterioration and little redevelopment, whether privately or publicly funded. At the other extreme, excessive demand over supply gives rise to homelessness, multi-occupation and overcrowding. Our preliminary work and that of others suggests that vacancy rates, homelessness and residential density are all basic factors that contribute to housing stress and obsolescence.[1] These factors give, in a limited way, an aggregative measure of the relative efficiency with which households and housing stock are matched.

The resources available to any household located in a particular dwelling are of two kinds. Firstly, there are those physical resources contained within the dwelling — rooms, facilities, garden, garage etc. Secondly, there are those resources available outside the home within the locality as a whole — employment, services, amenities etc. The traditional view is that the location of households is primarily a function of the location of employment. If we ignore households who are not 'job tied', e.g. retired households, then the notion that job availability is the most significant external factor that may affect the balance between households and housing stock seems reasonable. This is particularly true for lower-income households. Factors other than employment may also be significant. The non-availability of transport, shops, schools, open space, social and leisure facilities etc., together with the negative resources of noise, visual intrusion, lack of amenities etc. may all contribute to decay and obsolescence.[2] There are indications that the trade-offs made by households between the resources contained within the dwelling and those afforded by location may be in a state of change. The 1971 Census shows an accelerating rate of migration out of the conurbations. It is not known whether this drift from the cities is caused largely by market forces or whether it is undertaken by choice as a result of fundamental changes in dwelling and locational preference.

Different types of dwelling, tenure and location will entail different levels and types of constraint over their occupants. For example, much of the privately rented furnished accommodation in urban locations is in poor environmental surroundings, it lacks basic facilities, it is in need of physical repair, it is in multi-occupation, it is overcrowded, but rents are high. This combination of housing circumstances clearly gives rise to a very severe set of constraints. In contrast, suburban owner-occupied dwellings at present entail relatively unconstrained housing situations. However, this dwelling type may exercise different degrees of constraint during the various phases of its physical life span and could give rise to problems in the future.

The socio-economic character of households has a marked influence over the types and degrees of housing constraint that are experienced. For example, if a large family in private rented accommodation is in a poor bargaining position due to low income and job status, then it is probable that this household's effective range of choice will be constrained to areas of stock in poor condition. Such households are often severely constrained by the cost of the journey to work, and consequently occupy areas of poor housing in central urban areas. In the case of the owner-occupier, income is again a major constraining factor since it ultimately determines the mortgage, maintenance and adaption costs that can be afforded.

The degree to which housing requirements are met by the existing housing stock, i.e. the relationship between demand and supply, is conditional on the state of the local housing market. Market conditions give rise to different sets of constraints and opportunities in different housing areas, e.g. structurally identical houses sell at different prices due to locational factors and differences in the pressures of demand. Local authority dwellings may have similar rent levels but be of different ages, qualities and types. Within each tenure group, households face externally imposed constraints over and above the directly constraining influences imposed by their particular dwelling and the individual character of their household. The effects of the housing market on the process of obsolescence have been explored, in the past, through the concept of filtering. This was described in Chapter 2. The suggestion that the filtering model describes a natural process which can reduce the amount of poor housing and obsolescence among the lower-income groups is, we believe, fallacious. The market forces that result in poor households occupying poor dwellings also result in the reduction, and in extreme cases, the elimination, of the ability to move. In very poor housing areas the operation of market forces may be seen as one of the key factors in the continuation of severely obsolescent conditions.

The relationship between the housing market and general economic circumstances should also be mentioned. Construction in general, and housing in particular, play an important role in the national economy. In Britain some 15 per cent of private and 20 per cent of public capital formation is in dwellings. As long as there is a need for more houses — need being not only an economic consideration but also a social concept based on the right to good housing — the influence of the economy on the rate of house building and residential improvement, will have important implications for obsolescence.

We have now identified four sets of factors that contribute to the process of obsolescence. Firstly, there are 'internal' factors concerning the spatial, facility, physical and tenural characteristics of the stock, together with the socio-economic character of the inhabitants. Secondly, there are 'external' factors due to location: employment availability, proximity of transport, shops, schools, social amenities, leisure facilities, environmental nuisances etc. Thirdly, there are a number of circumstantial factors arising out of the nature of local housing markets. Finally, there are the effects of national economic circumstances, housing legislation, politics, policies and procedures.

The responses to obsolescence

At any point in time, there are three principal ways in which levels of obsolescence may increase or decrease: through absolute changes in the quantity and type of residential demand, through absolute changes in the supply of residential accommodation, and through relative changes resulting from the reallocation of households within the housing stock. These three types of change are reflected in the operations of the housing market and the interventions made to achieve a closer matching of housing supply to residential demand. At the level of the individual household, these three types of change are affected through the decisions 'to move' and 'to adapt' in the case of the owner-occupier, and 'to move' in the case of the tenant. These responses to obsolescence and the operations of the market will be discussed in turn.

Individual households can improve their housing conditions in two ways: by improving or adapting their current dwelling, and by moving home. Moving is the most common way in which households improve their residential conditions. During the last decade the yearly rate of household movement in Britain has been from 8 to 11 per cent. The proportion of households actively wishing to move at any given time has varied from 9 to 14 per cent.[3] Most studies of residential mobility have surveyed both past moving behaviour and present moving intentions. They have examined the reasons for moving and non-moving and the 'push–pull' factors involved. A review of post-war mobility surveys, both British and American, was completed during the early stages of our research. An inventory of reasons for moving and non-moving was compiled and the relative frequency with which these reasons occurred were examined. A consistent pattern was uncovered. It would appear that the expressed reasons for moving which are associated with housing factors are:

Reasons for moving

Size of dwelling, facilities, condition, sharing cost, tenure, and housing amenity

Reasons for non-moving

Size, cost and tenure

The social, employment and personal reasons for moving, while being somewhat independent of housing factors, were also important. For example, moves due to household formation, growth, fragmentation and retirement are an important component of the housing allocation process. Indirectly they may therefore be of considerable significance for obsolescence. Moving because of job availability or the journey to work may also contribute to the housing problems of an area. The general conclusions of our review of residential mobility surveys are listed below.

1   There was a consistent pattern in the reasons for moving. With the exception of only one survey's findings,[4] housing reasons predominated. The assumption that moving behaviour is strongly indicative of perceived housing conditions is validated by the published results of past mobility surveys.

2   In those cases where the decision to move has not been brought about by a single factor acting alone and where the principal purpose behind the move was not associated with housing, nevertheless the majority of households (some 70 per cent) took the opportunity offered by the move to improve their housing conditions.

3   Among the housing reasons given, the size of the accommodation was the most commonly experienced source of dissatisfaction.

4   Cost, as a stated reason for moving, rarely occurred. The results from all the mobility surveys reviewed were consistent in this respect. Had the surveys questioned more closely the reasons for non-moving, the results might have been rather different.

5   Households may either move to another dwelling in the same tenure or they may change tenure. There was no clear-cut picture of how tenancy inhibits or promotes mobility with the exception of the privately rented sector, which was characterised by a very high level of intending movers. In Britain the differences in average lengths of stay between local authority tenants and owner-occupiers are slight, but with much local variation.

6   Inter-tenure mobility is low. Moves from the public and privately rented sectors to owner-occupation are severely restricted, primarily by

income and house prices. Migration from owner-occupation to the rented sectors is also low, elderly households apart.

7   Age and household composition were important factors. The younger the head of household the greater the probability of moving, families with young children producing the peak mobility rates. The professional classes are more mobile, lower-income workers less so.

It is logical to expect that attitudes to residential movement should be largely determined by households weighing the advantages and disadvantages of their present accommodation against those in the expected future accommodation. But there would appear to be little evidence to support this 'decision theory' assumption. Little is known of the ways in which households perceive the opportunities open to them to improve their housing conditions.[5] A stated intention to move because of housing factors suggests two things: (i) dissatisfaction with the prevailing housing conditions, plus (ii) the perception that through moving the prevailing housing conditions could be improved. Moving, as an indicator of housing conditions, will tend to underestimate the severity of dissatisfaction since it will not account for those dissatisfied households who either do not perceive moving as an option open to them, or who cannot move for economic or personal reasons.

Owner-occupiers have the opportunity to adapt their dwelling in order to achieve improved housing conditions, provided of course that their location is satisfactory. In other tenure classes the choice to adapt generally belongs to the landlord, whether public or private. By-law application records show that a substantial proportion of owner-occupiers do make physical adaptions to their dwellings. However, in contrast to residential mobility, residential adaption is a poorly researched topic. Only two adaption surveys have been completed recently,[6],[7] and only the latter has been published. The general conclusions of that study were:

> . . . the type of people or households involved (in adaption) are those that are relatively young, usually with children, usually middle-class, with above-average incomes, most probably undertaking repairs and improvement in connection with a move. The houses involved are certainly not the oldest and tend to be of the period 1900—1940. While some may have lacked some amenities before improvement, most are already reasonably well equipped, tending to be the larger houses with gardens. The improvements are generally carried out in areas where the general standard of the residential environment is high and where the majority of houses in the area are well maintained and equipped with all amenities . . .

58

This published survey was, however, limited to the economic aspects of residential improvement. No motivational questions concerning the reasons for adapting or the choice between the responses of moving and adapting were included. Because of this, a survey of housing conversions and improvements in the owner-occupied sector was completed as part of our research. Within the very large range of physical changes that had been made, two major and two subsidiary reasons for adapting were discovered. The two most frequent and most important were 'to increase the size of the accommodation' and 'to modernise the dwelling'. The two main subsidiary reasons were 'to increase the value of the property' and 'preferred to adapt rather than move'. Details of this survey and its findings are summarised in Chapter 8.

The market framework

The housing market is closely related to the economy as a whole. General economic conditions have important effects on the building societies' ability to fulfil their role as the major source of finance in the owner-occupied sector. Two relationships should be mentioned: the effect of general economic conditions on the supply of funds to the building societies, and the effect of these conditions on the demand for loans.

Building societies compete for their funds with other forms of investment, particularly with the market in equities. During a period of price inflation, investors are likely to adjust their portfolios and substitute towards industrial shares since the increasing price of products improves the likelihood of higher profits and greater dividends in the short term. A second consideration is that the increasing capital value of the assets that the investor has helped to finance leads to the possibility of a capital gain being received by equity holders. Generally, building societies cannot compete with this sort of situation.

In periods of credit restraint some savers are likely to run down their deposits in order to finance present consumption. Apart from the net inflow of investors' deposits, the most important source of funds for building-society lending is capital repayment on existing mortgages which can be used in turn to finance new mortgages. In times of credit restraint such repayments tend to fall to a level around that agreed as a minimum by both parties when the mortgage was taken out. The funds available for new lending are therefore reduced. In the recent economic situation, with profits squeezed, capital investment low, high wage inflation and the future levels of demand uncertain, industrial shares were a risky form of investment. In these circumstances, building societies offered secure and attractive rates of interest. At the same time, fear regarding future employment prospects can encourage some precautionary saving by the general public. To summarise, it seems to be a reasonable generalisation that the flow of funds to building societies tends to be anti-cyclical, i.e. they tend to be plentiful in a recession. On the other hand the demand for loans tends to be pro-cyclical — higher in times of rising incomes and buoyant expectations.

A period of tight credit affects not only the building society and the public but also the builder who is likely to be suffering both a cut-back in the effective demand for his houses, due to credit difficulties on the demand side, as well as credit difficulties of his own. Many small and medium-sized builders rely on short-term bank credit which in times of restraint is likely to be frozen. These supply constraints explain why an increase in building-society lending does not always result in an increasing level of building activity. These credit constraints on both the demand and supply side will have a lagged effect on the actual supply of houses (as opposed to housing starts) due to work in hand and the staggering of completions.

Having touched on the importance of the housing and construction industry in the context of the economy as a whole, we shall examine the role of the housing market in causing obsolescence. Any assessment of the market's role in the creation of obsolescent stock must distinguish between the effects of free-market operations *per se* and the results of intervention in the market. The operation of a free housing market would result in the provision of different qualities of housing according to consumer preferences and relative abilities to pay.[8] In the absence of intervention or subsidy the distribution of income and wealth would determine the allocation of available stock to households. In free housing markets the major cause of poor housing conditions is low income[9] and only a change in the amount and distribution of income can fundamentally improve housing conditions. Foreign examples clearly show the detremental effects of a free market for low-income groups.[10]

In Britain the housing market has been subject to increasing degrees of intervention. Nevertheless 'a stock of typically old, worn housing, cut up in the process of downward conversion in order to decrease the size of the dwelling unit, is the type of accommodation that the housing industry provides to the poor'.[11] At any point in time the choices open to a household are restricted by the range of prices or rents of dwellings on offer, relative to their household income. Legislative housing standards and the rising cost of land, labour and materials have put new unsubsidised

60

dwellings beyond the reach of the less well off. Those market forces and market interventions that reduce the range and number of dwellings available to particular household types limit the ability of those households to improve their housing conditions by moving. In this respect the market framework and housing policies both contribute to increasing degrees of obsolescence. The relative influence of market operations and government interventions in alleviating or accentuating the problem of obsolescence should therefore be examined.

Such considerations are usually included within the study of 'externalities'. In the context of housing obsolescence, externalities may be described as those effects that result in private costs or benefits, disadvantages or advantages, for individual households, that arise out of external factors whether they be caused by the actions of other households, housing policies or financial and market forces as a whole. If housing decisions are taken in a particular area or sector in the light of that area's interest alone, and third party or 'social costs' are ignored, it may follow that such decisions as co-ordinated by the market will not lead to optimum economic conditions since all relevant effects have not been considered and priced, e.g. the external effects of housing stock in which a sizeable proportion of the houses are of a relatively poor quality, can be seen, for example, in the medical and social service expenditure incurred as a result, at least in part, of inadequate housing provision. More generally, poor housing appears to contribute to the probability of juvenile delinquency, truancy, vandalism, crime and mental illness, all of which may have harmful effects on both non-slum and slum dwellers alike.[12]

The externality concept can be used to examine the broader implications of the market framework on housing obsolescence. It is clear that the onset of obsolescence is not simply a result of the activities of irresponsible landlords, property speculators or poor households.[9] As dwellings become older their ability to fulfil the current requirements of their occupants decreases, yet most dwellings can be adequately maintained or improved at reasonable cost. Thus one would expect some rationale for the action of those landlords who find it profitable to allow dwellings to enter a spiral of decay and neglect.[7] Apart from the cases where the income of the owners, or the tenants' ability to pay prohibits adequate maintenance, the externalities imposed on dwellings and their owners have important effects.

Three examples can be given. Firstly, it is well known that the introduction of factories or motorways close to residential areas depresses the value of residential property,[13] thus making improvement or maintenance expenditure less worthwhile. Similarly, the fear that a property will be

61

compulsorily purchased or encroached upon by neighbouring land-users will reduce the desire to maintain the dwelling. Secondly, given that housing supplied for rent in the private sector is a form of investment, any control on the returns on this investment in a market economy may result in a reduction of the quantity of rented dwellings that are provided, and in a reduction in their quality, as owners attempt to minimise short-run expenditure. Given that the demand for rented dwellings remains high, units of accommodation may be subdivided to provide more units of accommodation but to poorer standards. Thirdly, the effects of the quality of surrounding dwellings may reduce expenditure on individual dwellings. The value of an individual property is partly related to the character and quality of the surrounding dwellings. In an area of poor stock, all owners could increase the value of their dwellings by improving them — gaining both from the increase in the value of their improved property and from the improvement of the surrounding area as a whole. However, if the majority of owners improve, an individual can gain by not improving at all and simply receiving an increase in the value of his dwelling as a result of the actions of other owners. Since this response is rational for all owners, and since the worst situation for the individual is for him to improve and for no one else to do so, there will be a tendency for no one to improve. Thus, as a result of externalities imposed by one dwelling on another, it is possible for a residential area to remain in a poor physical and environmental state until private or public redevelopment becomes unavoidable.

In conclusion, it can be seen that the operation of the market in response to a given income distribution will result in the allocation of different qualities of housing among different income groups. In the main, the externalities associated with the operation of the housing market may tend to accentuate these physical differences in quality and induce differentiation and polarisation between housing areas.[14] A key role of the market, and of policy regarding the operation of the market, lies in its ability to facilitate the alleviation of obsolescence. A regulated housing market can help to increase the degree to which feasible responses, such as moving or adapting, are opened up to disadvantaged households.

Degrees of obsolescence

From our general description of housing obsolescence the following factors that can contribute to the relative disutility of dwellings can be identified:

62

1   The constraints imposed by the spatial, physical, financial and tenural character of individual items and areas of housing stock.
2   The constraints imposed by the socio-economic character of households and the nature of their demands and preferences.
3   The constraints due to locational factors — employment structure, local service facilities, amenities and disamenities.
4   The constraints due to market factors — supply, demand, price, rent, interest rates, competition and intervention, legislative and financial measures.
5   The moving and adapting behaviour of individual households.
6   The rates and types of reconditioning, rehabilitation and renewal of the housing stock, undertaken by public and private agencies.

The constraining factors (1 to 4 above) provide a practical way through which the relative severity of obsolescence can be evaluated. The actions that may be taken to reduce constraint (5 and 6 above) will tend to depend not so much on the actual degrees of housing constraint, but rather on the constraints that are perceived to be operating. The perception of constraint, levels of discrimination and tolerance will probably vary with the age and type of perceiver. This subjective aspect gives rise to a number of well-known difficulties.

   First there is the problem, common in the social sciences, of distinguishing between preference and habit. Improved conditions of a general type with which the public is already familiar are usually more acceptable than those of a more novel kind. Advantages and disadvantages that are voiced may arise out of prejudice and past conditioning. Some households may see themselves as more constrained than they actually are, others may undervalue the constraints that they are experiencing. A considerable degree of tolerance may be apparent, varying with type of household and with type of constraint. Nevertheless, with such reservations in mind, certain boundaries between 'acceptable' and 'unacceptable' degrees of constraint can be detected. These boundaries can be defined statistically via the levels of constraint at which conditions are judged to cross the 'just-acceptable/just-unacceptable' threshold. Three primary levels of constraint can be distinguished in the case of households that have the ability to move from or adapt their dwellings.

1   Unacceptable level of constraint — complaint voiced and action taken, or shortly to be taken, to rectify.
2   Just-tolerable level of constraint — complaints made but no alleviating action taken or firmly planned.
3   Acceptable level of constraint — no complaint voiced and no action planned.

A simple view of this disutility scale is shown in Figure 4.1. It consists of a number of subscales, one for each component of disutility within the areas identified as potentially constraining.

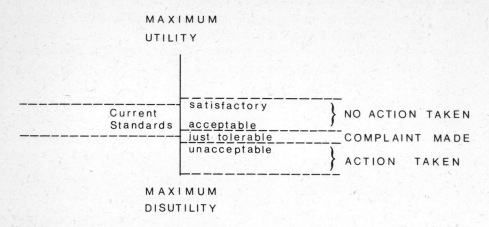

Figure 4.1   Disutility scale

It is clear that a significant proportion of households who are highly dissatisfied with their housing circumstances may not be able to do anything to improve their conditions, perhaps because of their location or, more probably, due to financial limitations. We must distinguish between a household's 'wish' and 'ability' to improve its accommodation. Within a strictly economic view, those households without the ability to improve their dwellings will be deriving the most satisfaction or the least dissatisfaction, from their rather highly constrained circumstances and the limited range of opportunities available to them. This may seem to imply that poor conditions suit the poorer households and that virtually none of the housing stock is truly obsolescent. On the other hand, from a social welfare point of view, poor conditions should be improved if they are not socially or environmentally acceptable to the minimum standards set by our society. Given relatively severe constraint, where there is evidence that those households that were able to act to reduce their constraints have done so, and there are clear indications that the remaining households are dissatisfied but financially unable to act, then their housing conditions may properly be classified in category 1 — unacceptable.

Through such definitions it is possible to begin to distinguish between degrees of constraint. An assessment of housing obsolescence in a particular area should make quantitative estimates of the tolerable, just-tolerable and intolerable levels of constraint. Degrees of constraint are assessed in a relatively unambiguous and explicit manner through the actions taken, to be taken, or not to be taken.

Our introductory remarks concerning housing obsolescence may now be summarised. The principal characteristic of our approach has been the view of obsolescence as a process — a process in which an identified set of housing constraints becomes progressively tighter and more unacceptable with time. Three aspects of this process are fundamental to an understanding of obsolescence: the potentially constraining factors themselves, the actions or responses that can be taken to reduce constraint, and the market framework. The responses that indicate dissatisfaction with housing conditions include the occupier's intention to move from, or adapt his dwelling. It follows, that for a particular type or class of dwelling, the degree of constraint is indicated by the proportion of those who express dissatisfaction relative to those who do not. The degree of housing obsolescence in an area will depend on the incidence and impact of constraint and response on the allocation of households to dwellings within the housing market. In the next chapter we shall consider the ways in which these assessments of housing constraint and obsolescence may be made.

Notes

[1] Greater London Council, *Demographic, Social and Economic Indices for wards in Greater London,* Occasional paper no. 3, March 1970.

[2] D.F. Medhurst and J. Parry Lewis, *Urban Decay: An Analysis and Policy,* Macmillan, London 1969.

[3] M. Woolf, *Housing Survey in England and Wales,* Government Social Survey, HMSO, London 1967.

[4] South Hampshire Technical Unit, 'South Hampshire Mobility Survey', summarised in unpublished report, 1970.

[5] A. Murie, *Household Movement and Housing Choice,* Occasional paper no. 28, Centre for Urban and Regional Studies, University of Birmingham, 1974.

[6] Department of Architecture, Liverpool University, A survey of house adaptions made during research sponsored by the Rowntree Trust, unpublished, 1968.

[7] R.M. Kirwan and D.B. Martin, *The Economics of Urban Residential Renewal and Improvement,* Working paper no. 77, Centre for Environmental Studies, London 1972.

[8] F.G. Penance and W.A. West, *Housing Market Analysis and Policy,* paper no. 48, Institute of Economic Affairs, 1969.

[9] R.F. Muth, *Cities and Housing,* University of Chicago Press, 1969.

[10] J.F.C. Turner and R. Fichter, *Freedom to Build,* London, Collier-Macmillan, 1972.

[11] J. Rothenberg, *Economic Evaluation of Urban Renewal,* The Brookings Institution, Washington 1967.

[12] Liverpool Corporation, Social Malaise in Liverpool, Internal Report, Undated.

[13] H.W. Richardson, *Urban Economics*, Penguin, Harmondsworth, Middlesex, 1971.

[14] D. Harvey, *Social Justice and the City,* Edward Arnold, London 1973.

5 The analysis of housing obsolescence

The central task in the analysis of obsolescence is to distinguish between the conditions that are 'just satisfactory' and those that are 'just unsatisfactory', the boundary between acceptable and unacceptable degrees of constraint imposed by the dwelling, its environment and the housing market. In housing, three distinct types of appraisal are common: those made by the occupants, those made by developers and landlords, and those made by local authority and government officers, politicians and public opinion generally. In our study, we are primarily concerned with the first type of appraisal, that made by the occupants themselves.

Individual households may express dissatisfaction with their housing conditions in three ways: they may move, they may improve or adapt their dwelling if they are owner-occupiers, or they may indicate dissatisfaction through complaint. The degree of obsolescence can be gauged from the statistic describing the proportion of responses in each of these categories for each type of constraint. A serious imbalance between the services yielded by a dwelling and those required by its occupants will give rise to an unacceptable level of constraint. An estimation of the degree of obsolescence through the assessment of constraint levels, will therefore involve:

1 The identification of the critical level of each type of constraint for each class of household.
2 The assessment of the occurrence of constraints in combination and the criticality of individual constraint levels in respect to all others both within and between household classes.
3 An account of the effects of different degrees and combinations of constraint on moving and adapting behaviour and an examination of the reallocation of households to dwellings which might result.

Stages 1 and 2 investigate those factors that give rise to obsolescence, while stage 3 analyses the factors that limit or expand the possibilities for remedial action. We shall now discuss these three stages in the analysis of obsolescence and the methodological problems which are involved.

The analysis of constraint

The analysis of constraint incorporates two basic components: the constraining factors and the actions that may be taken to reduce constraint. If C represents a set of potentially constraining factors, c_i; $i=1, \ldots, n$ — and A represents a set a_j; $j=1, \ldots, m$ — of possible actions or responses, then the framework for the analysis of the pattern of housing constraint is illustrated by the array:

$$
\begin{array}{l}
c_1 a_1, c_1 a_2, \ldots, c_1 a_m \\[1ex]
c_2 a_1, c_2 a_2, \ldots, c_2 a_m \\
\vdots \qquad \vdots \qquad\qquad \vdots \qquad = c_i a_j \\
c_n a_1, c_n a_2, \ldots, c_n a_m
\end{array}
$$

The steps in the analysis of constraint are typically:

1 The identification of sets of classes in C and A subject to the limitations of the data that are available, distinguishing those classes for which a statistical approach is possible.

2 A univariate analysis of constraint through the examination of individual elements, $c_i a_j$, in the array, that is the relationship between individual areas of constraint and particular types of response.

3 A multivariate analysis of constraint through the examination of each column $c_i a_j$; $i=1, \ldots, n$ — to investigate the relative influence of different constraints on one type of response. The examination of each row, $c_i a_j$; $j=1, \ldots, m$ — to investigate the relative influence of one type of constraint across the range of possible responses. This multivariate analysis identifies the combinational occurrence of constraining factors and responses and the relative significance of individual types of constraint and response in respect to all others.

In our study the objective criteria used to assess dissatisfaction was a household's active intention to change or modify its accommodation. These criteria measure dissatisfaction as a binary response: 'dissatisfied' (moving or adapting), 'not dissatisfied' (not moving or not adapting). The results of a traditional social survey approach that evaluates conditions through expressed opinion, could also be interpreted as a binary response: 'satisfied', 'dissatisfied'. There are six responses which may be considered; either separately or in combination.

1 Not moving

2 Moving, the reason for moving including potentially constraining factor c_i

3   Moving, the reason for moving not including c_i
4   Not adapting
5   Adapting, the reason for adapting including factor c_i
6   Adapting, the reason for adapting not including factor c_i

A binary variable y_i may therefore be defined for the ith household, where $y_i=1$ if the household is moving or adapting, and $y_i=0$ otherwise. If there are n households, then the proportion of them that are taking action to reduce their dissatisfaction is given by:

$$\text{prob } (A) = \sum_{i=1}^{n} \frac{y_i}{n}$$

The purpose of the analysis is to identify those constraining variables which are associated with the intention to move or adapt. We also wish to identify the more critical constraints, those that give rise to high values of prob (A). The analysis assumes that, in the absence of the effects that we are considering (i.e. the different levels of constraint), the probability of any particular household acting is constant. This assumption is justified when households are classified into reasonably homogeneous groups. If y_i is treated as a dependent variable then:

$$E(y_i) = \text{prob } (y_i=1) = \theta_i : \text{prob } (y_i=0) = 1 - \theta_i$$

and the problem can be expressed as one of investigating the dependence of θ_i on a set of independent variables.

The set of potentially constraining factors, C, are defined as binary or continuous variables. By definition each area of potential constraint, c_i, is a function of one of three classes of variable:

1   The set of physical-stock variables, P. These describe the physical characteristics of particular dwellings or areas of housing, for example the number of rooms, structural condition, presence of bath, sink, wc, kitchen, garden, garage, hot water, central heating, etc.
2   The set of household variables, B. These describe the characteristics of individual households or populations, for example the type, size, age and composition of households, their social class, income, etc.
3   The set of housing-situation variables, S. Housing-situation variables uniquely describe the state of affairs that arises when a particular household occupies a particular dwelling. They are therefore composed of both physical variables in P and behavioural variables in B. Examples would include the number of persons per room, the degree of sharing, a household's length of stay in a dwelling, housing costs expressed as a percentage of income.

Univariate approach

We shall consider the univariate case first where the influence of constraining variables are considered one at a time. The simplest form of univariate analysis occurs when the independent variable describes some characteristic of P, B or S as being either present or absent. That is, when the potentially constraining factor is described by a binary variable, e.g. the lack or presence of a fixed bath or whether the dwelling is shared or not. When binary variables are used the sample is divided into two groups, those that have the characteristic in question and those that do not. In each of the two groups some households will want to move (y_i=1) and some will not (y_i=0). If the constraint that we are considering has an effect on the decision to move or adapt then we shall expect the proportion of values y_i=1 and y_i=0 to be significantly different for the two groups. The situation may be simply represented as a 2 X 2 contingency table.

Table 5.1

The analysis of binary constraints

	Group 1	Group 2	Total sample
	Situations with characteristic c_i	Situations without characteristic c_i	
Households wishing to move: $Y=1$	A_1	A_2	A_1+A_2
Households not wishing to move: $Y=0$	n_1-A_1	n_2-A_2	$(n_1+n_2)-(A_1+A_2)$
Totals per group	n_1	n_2	n_1+n_2
Proportion for whom $Y=1$	$\dfrac{A_1}{n_1}$	$\dfrac{A_2}{n_2}$	$\dfrac{A_1+A_2}{(n_1+n_2)}$

The effect of the potential constraining factor c_i on the propensity to respond, in this case to move, will be revealed by the difference between $\dfrac{A_1}{n_1}$ and $\dfrac{A_2}{n_2}$. Statistically, the problem is one of estimating both the significance and confidence limits of this difference. In order to justify representing binary data in this simple way, two important assumptions must be fulfilled. Membership of groups 1 or 2 by a particular household must be independent of the group to which every other household belongs.

Secondly, there should be no other factors which affect the value taken by y_i. Of these two conditions the first may be satisfied by taking a random sample of households, but it is unlikely that the second condition will ever be satisfied fully. Conclusions based on this form of analysis alone should be interpreted with considerable caution.

We shall next consider the case where the independent variable may take one of a range of values. This is the case when the potentially constraining factor is a continuous variable. Here a rather different form of analysis is necessary. If we consider the response – moving or not moving – then for each potential constraint c_i, the number of households wishing to move, and those not wishing to move, can be plotted against the values of c_i. Median and quartile values may be calculated and compared. Distributions of the form shown in Figure 5.1 result. Here, $(n_1 - A_1)$ is the distribution of households not wishing to move and (A_1) is the distribution of households who do want to move. The probabilities of a household wishing to move may also be estimated for various ranges of the constraining factor. Points of inflexion and the gradients of the resultant cumulative-probability curve describe the form of the effects of individual constraints on the propensity to move. These distributions are purely descriptive. Since the scale of each c_i will employ different units, only the forms of the distributions may be compared between one type of constraint and another. The constraint scales for each c_i may be partitioned so that the probabilities within each partition are as similar as possible. Consequently, the boundaries between partitions will occur where significant changes in probability values indicate what may be called 'critical' constraint thresholds.

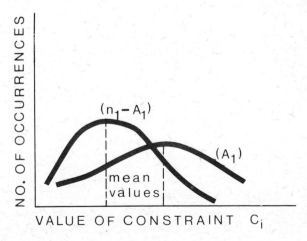

Figure 5.1   Distributions of moving and non-moving households

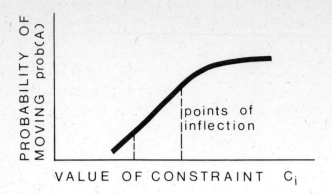

Figure 5.2   Probability of moving

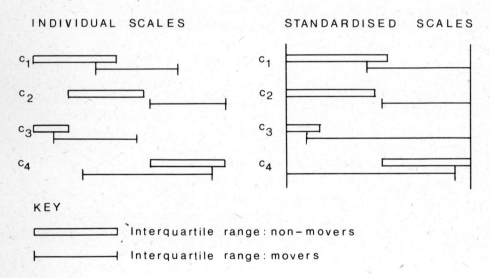

KEY

Figure 5.3   Constraint scales

Irrespective of the units in which c_i is measured, the extremities of the interquartile ranges of c_i for movers and non-movers can be set up on a standard scale, as illustrated in Figure 5.3. For each factor the percentage of the 'non-moving' interquartile range which is covered by the 'moving' interquartile range could be interpreted as an indication of the relative criticality of that factor. For example, factor c_4 has about 65 per cent of its moving interquartile range covered. Since about 30 per cent of the non-moving households have the same values of c_4 as do the moving households, it would appear that there is considerable tolerance of constraint c_4. This sort of interpretation must be treated cautiously since it relates only to the effect of one constraint on the probability of moving, while the effects of other variables may be present. However, by comparing these distributions, it is possible to describe ranges for each constraint which reveal significant differences between moving and non-moving groups. The degree to which these ranges overlap, indicates an area within which the constraint values are just tolerable.

Multivariate approach

Many of the variables used in a description of potential constraint are inter-correlated. We are usually faced with a situation where the probability of a household moving or adapting within a specified time period is dependent on a number of different factors. Relations of this kind may be investigated through standard regression and factorial design techniques. Following a review of various techniques a type of multiple regression analysis was selected for our empirical work as being most suitable for the analysis of housing constraints.

The aims of the multivariate analysis are twofold. Firstly, to assess the effects of combinations of constraining factors on the desire to move and the desire to adapt, and secondly, to develop a methodology for predicting the propensity of different household types to move and adapt given any particular set of housing circumstances. Put simply, the analysis allows for the combined effect of two (or more) independent variables on the dependent variable by introducing a composite variable composed of these two independent variables. Essentially, this allows for the possibility of the effect of two variables occurring together being greater than the sum of their effects if occurring singly. As in the univariate approach the dependent variable is a surrogate indicator of response to constraint, defined as a binary variable, taking the values zero or one according to whether the household intended to move or not, or adapt or not. Many of the independent variables in the set of potentially constraining factors are measured on a nominal scale; these are transformed to binary variables.[1] We will use a simple example to describe the basic principle of this approach.[2],[3] Consider just two characteristics of a housing situation; fitness of the dwelling, and occupancy rate, measured in persons per room (ppr). We might define states for these variables to get:

(1) Fitness of dwelling: S1 — unfit
  S2 — fit

(2) Occupancy rate: S1 — less than 0·5 ppr
  S2 — 0·5 to 0·9 ppr
  S3 — over 0·9 ppr

Three binary dummy variables can be defined to specify all possible values of these characteristics: $X2$, $X3$ and $X4$ in the table below corresponding to S1/S2 in variable (1) and S1/S2 in variable (2). It is not necessary to define a variable for S3 since any resulting equation will show the effect of S3 on the dependent variables simply by setting $X3$ and $X4$ equal to zero. Any other procedure would lead to the equation being over-determined. Multiplicative interactions between these three binary variables can be defined by a further two variables, $X5$ and $X6$, where

$$X5 = X2 . X3 \text{ and } X6 = X2 . X4$$

These interactions are illustrated in Table 5.2.

Table 5.2

Definition of binary variables

Fitness of dwelling	Occupancy rate	Binary dummy variables				Interaction variables	
		$X1$	$X2$	$X3$	$X4$	$X5$	$X6$
S1	S1	1	1	1	0	1	0
S1	S2	1	1	0	1	0	1
S1	S3	1	1	0	0	0	0
S2	S1	1	0	1	0	0	0
S2	S2	1	0	0	1	0	0
S2	S3	1	0	0	0	0	0

The variable $X1$ is included in order to provide a constant term but in practice most multiple regression packages, including that used in our analysis, generate a constant term automatically. The variables $X5$ and $X6$ indicate the effects of particular states of the other variables interacting together. For example, we can expect the effects of particular levels of unfitness and occupancy rate occurring together to be greater than the simple sum of the effects occurring separately which is the usual assumption in non-interactive regression analyses. Thus we can postulate a relationship of the form: $Y = \beta_1 X_1 + \beta_2 X_2 + \beta_3 X_3 + \beta_4 X_4 + \beta_5 X_5 + \beta_6 X_6$.

74

Now if $E(Y \mid 1, 2)$ is the expected value of Y when the dwelling is in fitness-state 1 and the occupancy rate is in state 2, then

$$E(Y \mid 1, 2) = \beta_1 + \beta_2 + \beta_4 + \beta_6$$

and if the observations of Y are binary as defined before, then $E(Y \mid 1, 2)$ can be interpreted as the probability that a household living in an unfit dwelling at an occupancy rate between 0·5 and 0·9 ppr will want to move from their present dwelling, i.e. the probability that $Y=1$.

It is important to distinguish between interaction effects and multi-colinearity. The latter refers to the high correlation between explanatory variables which makes the estimation of their separate effects difficult. The former refers to the additional effect which the occurrence of two explanatory variables has by virtue of their occurrence together, thus improving the precision of estimates. In practice, the combinations of binary constraints can only take one of two values (1 or 0) and hence will tend to yield higher degrees of multicolinearity than the linear combi-nations of continuous variables. In our multivariate analysis of housing constraint, 10 or more characteristics have been investigated at a time, with an extensive range of first-order interactions using a stepwise mul-tiple regression to introduce binary dummy variables one at a time. Clearly as more characteristics are added they may interact 3, 4 or more at a time. However as the higher-order interactions generate an unmanageable number of additional variables which become difficult to interpret, we have limited our investigation to interactions between pairs of dummy variables. The results of this analysis will be described in Chapter 6.

A simulation model

In order to describe housing obsolescence we must be able to relate the 'constraint and response' approach to the wider study of the process of change that takes place at the interface between dwellings and households. Beginning with an inventory of households, dwellings and housing situ-ations, we need to be able to follow the changes that take place over time. We need to monitor these changes in order to assess whether housing constraint is increasing or decreasing. We are particularly concerned with the allocation of households who are presently dissatisfied with their housing provisions, to types of dwelling and tenure that more closely meet their demands, with the proviso that households may only be allocated to dwellings that are both vacant and 'accessible' to them. We need to be able to simulate the proportion of currently dissatisfied households that could gain access to various dwelling types and their relative bargaining positions *vis-à-vis* other households who also wish to gain access. In this respect the concept of access criteria as introduced in Chapter 4 is particularly relevant.

The term 'access criteria' refers to those factors affecting the likelihood of a given household being admitted to a given unit of stock. They affect the allocation of households to stock in three important ways. Firstly, access constraints determine which households can compete for which dwelling/tenure types. Secondly, access constraints when defined in the widest sense to include bargaining power, help to differentiate between the four main stages of the allocation procedure: the desire to move, the general ability to move, the financial ability to gain access to a particular type of dwelling and the ability to secure one of the available vacancies in that class in competition with other households. Finally, access constraints permit the identification of the set of frustrated households, i.e. those who wish to move or adapt and hence improve their housing circumstances, but who are unable to do so due to market conditions.

The general aim of our housing-simulation model is to describe and monitor the effects of the allocation of households to stock, and to evaluate the long-term repercussions that such allocations might have on the degree and rate of obsolescence. The simulation does not attempt to model the housing market *per se,* neither does it aim to achieve a general housing model. It concentrates on those aspects of housing conditions, housing mobility and the operations of the housing market that are directly relevant to obsolescence. Changes in government policy and alternative local authority actions cannot be modelled explicitly. Such factors, together with changing values and standards of housing expectations, must be treated exogenously. The initial factors bringing about household change, for example birth and death rates, the rate of household formation and migration etc., must also be considered as exogenous. The rates of housebuilding and demolition, together with policies concerning rehabilitation and renewal must be similarly treated. It is the possible consequence of exogenous changes of these kinds on the distribution of households among stock, and the incidence and degrees of obsolescence that this entails, that is the central concern of our simulation model. Finally, the simulation model supplements – rather than duplicates – the existing demographic, house condition, financial and economic housing models.[4] The framework of the simulation model is illustrated in Figure 5.4. Various components of the model will be discussed in turn.

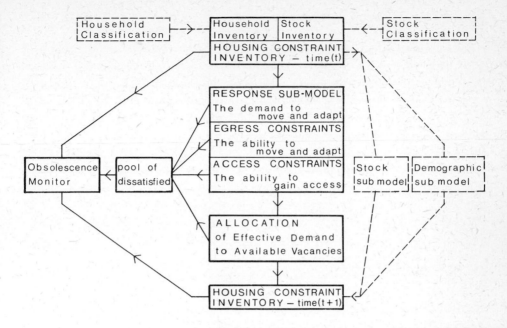

Figure 5.4   Structure for a simulation model

Households, dwellings and housing situations

A description of housing conditions will cover four basic circumstances: individual households occupying individual dwellings, dwellings shared by two or more households, homeless households and vacant dwellings. Households and dwellings must first be classified. The objective of the classification is to define homogeneous groups of stock and households so that within-group similarity is maximised and between-group similarity is minimised. The groups so defined should be multipurpose. They must provide a suitable basis for data description, for the analysis of constraint and for simulation, and if they are to assist implementation, they should relate to the stock and household categories currently used by government and local authorities.

Briefly, the classification is conceived as follows: if [B] is a set of behavioural attributes that are available in the data to describe households, and [P] is a set of physical attributes available to describe housing stock, then households can be classified into k classes through [B], and housing stock can be classified in l classes through $[P]$. Techniques for performing this type of classification, have been extensively reviewed by Everitt.[5] Three types of classification technique were considered: similarity analysis, dissimilarity analysis and factor analysis, similarity analysis being subsequently selected. After a comparison of the standard software packages, the cluster analysis program CLUSTAN was selected since it offered a choice of clustering methods and alternative clustering coefficients within the same program.[6] A further dimension to be included in the classification is that of tenure. This may be handled in one of two ways. The simulation could run separately for each tenure class, intertenural flows being handled exogenously. Alternatively, tenure can be included as one of the distinguishing attributes used to classify dwellings. The mathematical formulation that follows can accommodate either approach. Households, dwellings and housing situations are described as follows:

h_i is the number of households type i, where $i=1, \ldots k$. The total number of households $H = \sum_i h_i$

d_j is the number of dwellings type j, where $j=1, \ldots l$. The total number of dwellings $D = \sum_j d_j$

The number of unique housing situations is lk. In practice, many housing situations give rise to very similar degrees of constraint. These can be combined accordingly.

h_{ij} is the number of households type i occupying dwellings type j

d_{ji} is the number of dwelling type j occupied by households type i

Since two or more households may share an occupied dwelling $h_{ij} \geq d_{ji}$. The household occupancy rate is given by

$$w_{ij} = \frac{h_{ij}}{d_{ji}} \tag{5.1}$$

So the occupancy rate w_{ij} is defined as the average number of households type i per occupied dwelling type j, and is given by the total number of households of class i who are living in dwellings of class j, divided by the total number of dwellings of class j that are occupied by households of class i. By definition $w_{ij} \geq 1$.

Households without dwellings and dwellings without households are described as follows:

78

v_j is the number of vacant dwelling type j and the vacancy rate, V_j, is given by

$$V_j = 100 \cdot \frac{v_j}{d_j} \qquad (5.2)$$

z_i is the number of homeless households type i and the homelessness rate Z_i is given by

$$Z_i = 100 \cdot \frac{z_i}{h_i} \qquad (5.3)$$

The total number of households of type i is given by

$$h_i = \sum_{j=1}^{j=l} h_{ij} + z_i \qquad (5.4)$$

The total number of dwellings of type j is given by

$$d_j = \sum_{i=1}^{i=k} d_{ji} + v_j \qquad (5.5)$$

The average household occupancy rate W is given by

$$W = \frac{H - \sum_{i=1}^{i=k} z_i}{D - \sum_{j=1}^{j=l} v_j} \qquad (5.6)$$

Moving, egress and access

It is assumed that the desire to move, on the part of a particular household in a particular dwelling, depends on the relative unsuitability of the dwelling for that particular household, i.e. the desire to move is affected by the household's current 'housing situation'. Those households who move because of a change of job, in order to be nearer relatives and for a variety of other 'non-housing' reasons, are excluded from the present discussion. So for a particular household we can write:

$$\text{prob } (M) = f(c_x) \qquad (x = 1, \ldots n) \qquad (5.7)$$

where prob (M) is the probability that the household will want to move and c_x is a subset of potentially constraining factors C.

Because of the likelihood of heterogeneity even within similar household classes, there will be a range of values for each element c_x, for each ith class of household. If we consider the subclass of households living in dwellings of class j there would still be no unique value for each c_x, from which we can derive a unique estimate of the probability that a household of class i living in a dwelling of class j will want to move. There appear to be two ways we might represent the moving behaviour of the subclass. We either consider the individual values of c_x for each household, by calculating a set of values for prob (M) and taking the mean value as representative of the subclass. Alternatively, we might find the mean value of each c_x for the ijth housing situation, C_{ij}, in which case the probability of moving is given by

$$\text{prob } (M) = M_{ij} = f_{ij}(C_{ij}) \tag{5.8}$$

where M_{ij} is the probability of any household type i in dwelling type j wishing to move per unit time. The number of households wishing to move (m_{ij}) is given by

$$m_{ij} = M_{ij} \cdot h_{ij} \tag{5.9}$$

Similarly, the number of households in the owner-occupied sector wishing to adapt $(\bar{a}_{ij})$ is given by

$$\bar{a}_{ij} = \bar{A}_{ij} \cdot h_{ij} \tag{5.10}$$

where $\bar{A}_{ij}$ is the probability of a household type i in dwelling type j wishing to adapt or improve their dwelling during the current time period.

If Q_{ij} is the proportion of households h_{ij} who are financially able to move out of dwelling type j to a minimally improved housing situation, then the number who wish to and could move, q_{ij}, is given by

$$q_{ij} = Q_{ij} \cdot m_{ij} \tag{5.11}$$

If U_{ij} is the proportion of households h_{ij} who are financially able to adapt their dwelling type j to a minimally improved class, then the number who wish to and can adapt, u_{ij}, is given by

$$u_{ij} = U_{ij} \cdot \bar{a}_{ij} \tag{5.12}$$

If G_i^x is the proportion of households type i who could afford to gain access to dwellings type x, then the number of households who wish to and could afford to gain access to dwellings d_x is given by

$$g_{ij}^x = G_i^x \cdot q_{ij} \tag{5.13}$$

Substituting (5.9) and (5.11) in (5.13)

$$g_{ij}^x = G_i^x \cdot Q_{ij} \cdot M_{ij} \cdot h_{ij} \qquad (5.14)$$

Here g_{ij}^x represents the effective demand of h_{ij} for dwelling type x, where $x = (j + 1), \ldots l$ and is an input to the allocation submodel.

Three further expressions are important. The number, $\hat{q}_{ij}$, of households who wish to move and improve their housing conditions but cannot afford to do so is given by

$$\hat{q}_{ij} = h_{ij} M_{ij} (1 - Q_{ij}) \qquad (5.15)$$

The number, $\hat{m}_{ij}(q)$, of households who do not wish to move and improve their housing conditions but could afford to do so is given by

$$\hat{m}_{ij}(q) = h_{ij} Q_{ij} (1 - M_{ij}) \qquad (5.16)$$

The number, $\hat{m}_{ij}(\hat{q})$, of households who do not wish to move but also could not afford to move is given by

$$\hat{m}_{ij}(\hat{q}) = h_{ij} (1 - M_{ij}) (1 - Q_{ij}) \qquad (5.17)$$

Equations (5.15), (5.16) and (5.17) are inputs to the obsolescence monitor. Two important assumptions have been made in arriving at expressions (5.9) to (5.17). Firstly, homogeneous household and stock classifications are assumed. Secondly, the formulation implies that the probability of moving, M_{ij}, and the financial ability to move, Q_{ij}, can be calibrated independently. The equations relating the desire and ability to move, to actual moving behaviour are summarised in Figure 5.5.

Allocation procedures

Little is known about households' criteria for moving home and the typical decision processes that are involved. Given the financial ability to gain access, it is bargaining power and the workings of the market as a whole that determines which households acquire the vacant stock. Households compete not only for those dwellings offered at a price or rent equal to the maximum that they can afford, but also compete for stock currently offered at prices or rents which fall below this maximum. Those households that cannot secure a vacant dwelling towards their upper limit of expenditure may compete for cheaper accommodation and outbid those households whose ability to pay is lower. The housing market is highly imperfect however, and a rational bidding procedure cannot be assumed. Moreover the method of allocation differs from sector to sector.

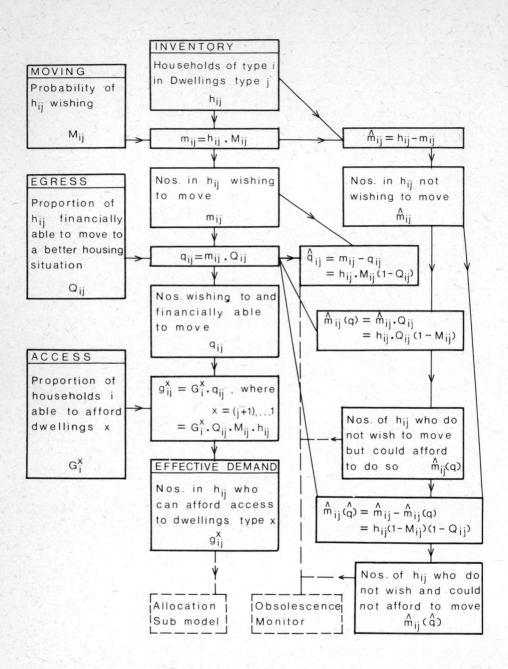

Figure 5.5   Moving, egress and access

For the purposes of the simulation a number of alternative behavioural assumptions concerning the allocation procedure could be assumed. Those households that have effective demand for a particular type of stock could be allocated to the existing vacancies in that type of stock, using random numbers. In contrast, households could be allocated strictly according to their relative bidding powers, a perfect-market assumption. We could make a 'crawling assumption' such that, during each time period, the maximum number of households make at least a minimal improvement in their housing conditions. Alternatively, households could be allocated to the available vacancies on a proportional basis within the limitations of specified economic constraints.

After reviewing a number of behavioural axioms that might have been employed, two were selected for detailed investigation. The first, allocation procedure A, is a linear programming formulation. This procedure rests on the simple theoretical assumption that households can be allocated at time (t) such that the demands for allocations at time $(t+1)$ are minimised. The second allocation procedure, B, rests on the assumption that households act only to 'reduce' their housing constraints over time. This is a pragmatic assumption concerning the way households take decisions with limited knowledge of the housing market. Neither assumption could be tested with the evidence available to us. These two allocation procedures will be described in turn.

Allocation procedure A

The total number of households type i who want to move is given by

$$m_i = \sum_{j=1}^{j=l} m_{ij} + z_i \qquad (5.18)$$

The number of dwellings of each type to which they could be allocated is given by

$$\overset{*}{v}_j = \sum_{i=1}^{i=k} \frac{m_{ij}}{w_{ij}} + v_j \qquad (j = 1, \ldots l) \qquad (5.19)$$

where $\overset{*}{v}_j$ is the number of potential vacancies in the system, that is the total number of class j dwellings that households wish to leave plus those already vacant. The actual movement of households into stock is constrained by market and other factors which must be taken into account. If we define N_i^j as the number of households of class i who wanted to move at time (t) and who are allocated to a dwelling of class j by time $(t+1)$, we can formalise a number of constraints acting on these N_i^j. Those households who were living in a dwelling of class j at time t can either be considered not to have succeeded in moving, or to have moved within the class j. Our interest is in inter-class movements since this is what affects the distribution of households between dwelling types. It is not necessary, therefore, to distinguish between intra-class movement and failure to move.

The number of allocated households at $(t+1)$ cannot exceed the effective demand at (t). Similarly the number of households allocated to dwellings type j cannot exceed the number of available dwellings type j. So

$$\sum_{j=1}^{j=l} N_i^j + z_i^{(t+1)} \leqslant \sum_{j=1}^{j=l} m_{ij} + z_i^{(t)} \tag{5.20}$$

$$\sum_{j=1}^{j=l} N_i^j + v_j^{(t+1)} \leqslant \sum_{i=1}^{i=k} \frac{m_{ij}}{w_{ij}} + v_j^{(t)} \tag{5.21}$$

The formulation of these two constraints could be modified to allow for positive or negative changes in the number of households and dwellings in each class. In our formulation the effects of inward and outward migration on the system being studied, together with other demographic changes, are treated as exogenous to the allocation procedure. Changes to the inventory of housing stock through demolition and new buildings are treated in the same way.

The influence of economic constraints on the allocation process was described earlier. In allocation procedure A, the simplest formulation is adopted. Since not all households type i are able to afford to gain access to dwellings type j, we define:

G_i^j — the proportion of households in class i who could afford to move into dwellings type j (in an ideal case where i and j are perfectly homogeneous classes then $G_i^j = (0, 1)$ for all i and j)

Then
$$N_i^j \leqslant G_i^j \left(\sum_{j=1}^{j=l} m_{ij} + z_i \right) \tag{5.22}$$

This expression generates a set of constraints arising from the distribution of the abilities to pay for each class of dwellings by individual households within each class of household. Provided there is a mean maximum annual sum, e_i, which a particular class of household i can afford to allocate to housing expenditure and a mean annual cost p_j of a dwelling in class j, then the following additional constraint can be incorporated:

$$\sum_{j=1}^{j=l} \sum_{i=1}^{i=k} N_i^j \cdot p_j \leqslant \sum_{i=1}^{i=k} e_i \cdot \sum_{j=1}^{j=l} m_{ij} \tag{5.23}$$

84

We need to find a set of values for N_i^j which satisfy the linear constraints imposed by the expressions and inequalities (5.18) to (5.21). Allocation procedure A assumes that, with other factors remaining constant, the N_i^j are chosen such that the number of households wanting to move at $(t+1)$ is minimised. Thus we find the values of N_i^j which minimise the expression:

$$\sum_{j=1}^{j=l} \sum_{i=1}^{i=k} M_{ij} N_i^j \qquad (5.24)$$

And

$$h_{ij}^{(t+1)} = h_{ij}^{(t)} (1 - M_{ij}) + N_i^j \qquad (5.25)$$

Allocation procedure B

Allocation procedure B rests on the assumption that, per unit time, the probability of transition from housing situation h_{ij} to h_{il} is dependent on five factors:

(i)   the desire to move of households class i in dwellings type j, m_{ij} from equation (5.9)
(ii)   the proportion of households class i in dwellings type j with the financial capability to move out of d_j to a minimally less constrained housing situation, q_{ij} from equation (5.11)
(iii)   the proportion of households class i who could afford to gain access to dwellings type l, G_i^l in equation (5.13)
(iv)   the supply of vacant dwellings v_l
(v)   the level of competition for vacant stock v_l

Given factors (i), (ii) and (iii), then the effective demand g_{ij}^l of households class i in dwellings type j for dwellings type l may be calculated using equation (5.14). Factors (iv) and (v) are the basic market constraints limiting successful allocation. The general procedure for matching effective demand to vacant supply is illustrated in Figure 5.6.

Dwellings are first ranked according to cost (purchase price in the case of the owner-occupied sector and annual rent in other cases) so that $p_{(l)} > p_{(l-1)} > p_{(l-2)} \ldots$. The demands for the most expensive type of dwelling in the tenure class are considered first. Households with effective demand for dwellings class l are allocated to vacancies v_l on a proportional basis. The probability of obtaining a vacancy is a function of (vacant supply ÷ effective demand) if the total demand exceeds supply. If supply exceeds demand then the probability of obtaining a vacancy is a function of (effective demand ÷ demand). The number of households, by type, that are allocated at each cycle of the iteration, are recorded. The newly created

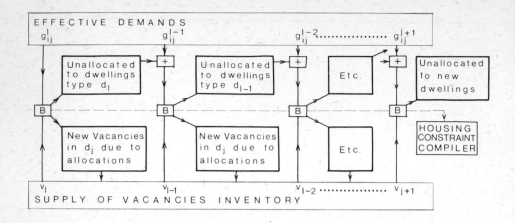

EFFECTIVE DEMANDS
g^l_{ij} g^{l-1}_{ij} g^{l-2}_{ij}................ g^{j+1}_{ij}

| Unallocated to dwellings type d_l | + | Unallocated to dwellings type d_{l-1} | + | Etc. | | + | Unallocated to new dwellings |

B — — — — B — — — — B — — — — B — — — →

HOUSING CONSTRAINT COMPILER

| New Vacancies in d_j due to allocations | | New Vacancies in d_j due to allocations | | Etc. | |

v_l v_{l-1} v_{l-2}................ v_{j+1}
SUPPLY OF VACANCIES INVENTORY

Figure 5.6   General method of allocation

vacancies arising from allocations to vacancies in class l are added to an inventory of vacancies. Those households that had effective demand for class l but were not allocated, are added to those having effective demand for class $l-1$. The procedure continues until all types of vacant stock and demand have been considered. This completes one iteration of the process. It is important to note that during this allocation procedure prices are fixed; while this may be reasonable for any individual household, it is clear that the effects of a large number of households bidding for a limited number of dwellings or a limited number of households bidding for a large number of dwellings would result in price changes in the owner-occupied and uncontrolled private rented sectors. It is possible to include such changes in two ways: firstly, by allowing prices to rise to a level marginally above the ability to pay of the 'second-best' bidder, or secondly, by revising prices upwards or downwards by an adjustment factor at the end of each iteration.

The allocation procedure — B in Figure 5.6 — which is carried out at each iteration, can be summarised by

$$N^l_{ij} = \frac{(v_l \cdot g^l_{ij})K}{\sum\limits_{i=1}^{i=k} \sum\limits_{j=1}^{j=l} g^l_{ij}} + L(g^l_{ij}) \qquad (5.26)$$

where $K = 1$ and $L = 0$ if $v_l < \sum\limits_{i=1}^{i=k} \sum\limits_{j=1}^{j=l} g_{ij}^l$ (5.27)

$K = 0$ and $L = 1$ if $v_l \geq \sum\limits_{i=1}^{i=k} \sum\limits_{j=1}^{j=l} g_{ij}^l$ (5.28)

where N_{ij}^l is the flow of households class i from housing situation h_{ij} at time (t) to housing situation h_{il} at time $(t+1)$

$\sum\limits_{i=1}^{i=k} \sum\limits_{j=1}^{j=l} g_{ij}^l$ is the total effective demand in the system for stock type l per unit time

K and L are binary dummy variables describing the two fundamental types of market conditions, when supply exceeds demand, and when demand exceeds supply

So that $$N_{ij}^l = I_{il}^{(t+1)} = O_{ij}^{(t+1)} \qquad (5.29)$$

where I_{il} and O_{ij} are the inputs and outputs from housing situations type il and ij respectively, that are recorded.

The unfilled vacancies $\hat{v}_l$ in stock type l at the end of the first cycle of iteration is given by

$$\hat{v}_l = v_l - \sum\limits_{i=1}^{i=k} \sum\limits_{j=1}^{j=l} N_{ij}^l \qquad (5.30)$$

With equations (5.26), (5.27) and (5.28) we can calculate the number of changes in each housing situation per iteration. The inability to respond by moving due to market conditions is given by

$$\hat{g}_{ij} = M_{ij} \cdot Q_{ij} \cdot h_{ij} - \sum\limits_{x=(j+1)}^{x=l} N_{ij}^x \qquad (5.31)$$

where $\hat{g}_{ij}$ is the total number of households class i in dwellings type j with effective demand to move that were unable to do so due to market conditions. This is one of the inputs to the obsolescence monitor. The equations involved in allocation procedure B are summarised in Figure 5.7.

Both of the allocation procedures A and B have been incorporated within a general simulation program. Program A requires approximately 200K of store and runs in less than 4 minutes' CPU time for all practical applications on the IBM 360. The program incorporating allocation procedure B requires approximately 120K of store and runs in less than 1 minute CPU time for all practical applications, and for most runs,

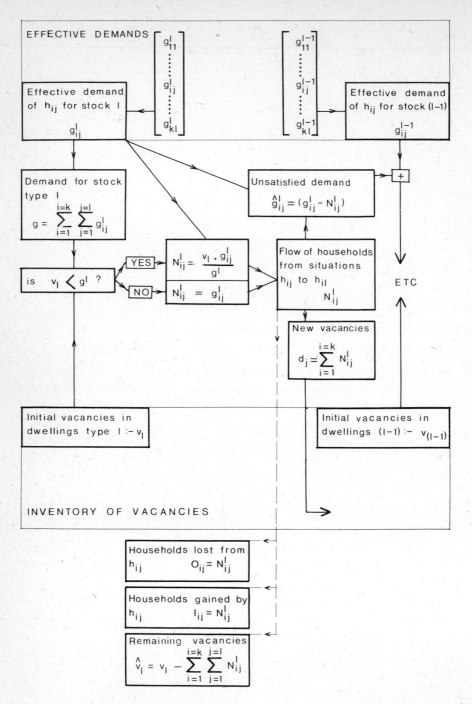

Figure 5.7   Allocation procedure (B)

less than 15 seconds of CPU time is required. The latter program is therefore more practically suited for implementation. Program descriptions and an example test run are included in Appendix A.

Monitoring housing conditions

Any deterioration or improvement in the overall levels of housing constraint can be monitored during simulation runs. Two basic characteristics are recorded — the number of households within each housing situation class at each iteration, and the number of households who, while wishing to respond and improve their housing conditions are unable to do so due to either the access constraints or to deficiencies in the supply of vacant stock. Four combinations of circumstance are possible:

A   Households who wished to respond (move or adapt) in order to improve their housing conditions and had the financial ability to do so

B   Households who wished to respond but did not have the financial ability to do so

C   Households who did not wish to respond but would have had the financial ability to do so if they so wished

D   Households who did not state a wish to respond but who were also financially unable to respond.

An identical breakdown by type of response can be applied in the case of adapting behaviour. The proportion wishing to move to improve their housing conditions is given by the simple ratio $(A + B)/(C + D)$, the higher the value the greater the level of dissatisfaction with current housing conditions. Two further ratios are important. The ratio $B/(A + B)$ gives the proportion of frustrated potential movers, the higher the value the less the likelihood that current constraint levels will be relaxed and housing conditions improved. The ratio $D/(C + D)$ gives the proportion of nonmovers who do not have the ability to move to better housing conditions, again the higher the value the lower the potential for improvement. Coincident low values in all three ratios is the only combination that certainly indicates satisfactory housing conditions. These ratios are used in our simulation model, to help monitor levels of housing obsolescence. The form of the output from the monitor at each iteration is as follows:

(i)   the number of households per housing-situation class $[H]^{(t)} \times [D]^{(t)}$

(ii)   total number of vacant dwellings $v_D{}^{(t)} = \sum\limits_{j=1}^{j=l} v_j$

total number of homeless households $z_H{}^{(t)} = \sum\limits_{i=1}^{i=k} z_i$

(iii)   the inabilities to respond as described through $\hat{q}$, $q\hat{m}$, and $\hat{q}\hat{m}$ from equations (5.15), (5.16) and (5.17) respectively

Print-outs may also include 'tables of differences' and proportional distributions as required, together with vacancy-rate and occupancy-rate tables.

Notes

[1] D.B. Suits, 'Use of dummy variables in regression equations', *American Statistical Association Journal,* vol. 52, December 1957, pp. 548–51.

[2] J. Johnston, *Econometric Methods,* McGraw-Hill, New York 1963.

[3] G.H. Orcutt, M. Greenberger, J. Korbel and A.M. Riulin, *Microanalysis of Socio-economic Systems: A Simulation Study,* Harper and Row, New York 1961.

[4] PTRC Symposium, *Housing Models,* Planning and Transport Research and Computation Co. Ltd, London, February 1970.

[5] B. Everitt, *Cluster Analysis,* Heinemann, London 1974.

[6] Wishart, 1969 CLUSTAN 1A, Cluster Analysis Program prepared at the Computing Laboratory, University of St Andrews.

PART 3

Applications

6 Housing constraint and obsolescence

Essentially, the degree of housing obsolescence depends on the needs and requirements of households for dwellings. Any action that implies that a household is seriously dissatisfied with its accommodation can, we believe, be a reliable indicator that the current level of housing constraint as perceived by that household is unacceptable. In this — the third and final section — we shall describe some of the results of our empirical studies of housing constraint and obsolescence. First, we have to calibrate those levels of housing constraint at which households decide to act, either by seeking alternative accommodation, or by adapting their dwellings.

One possible objection to this approach has been mentioned earlier. Many households who are experiencing intolerable levels of constraint may be unable to move or adapt and they could therefore be confused with those households who are actually satisfied with their conditions. Indeed, it may be argued that if all those households who found their current dwellings obsolescent were able to move or adapt, the major problem of obsolescence would be the removal of unoccupied dwellings no longer required. Clearly this is not the case. The market implications of obsolescence must also be considered, i.e. the nature of a second set of constraints which limit the ability of households to respond to poor housing conditions. Three aspects of constraint and response need therefore to be examined.

1 The levels of constraint perceived by households and the characteristics of those households who wish to move as compared to those who do not wish to move (hereafter termed 'movers' and 'non-movers' respectively).
2 The socio-economic and institutional constraints affecting the ability to move and the ability to adapt.
3 The levels of constraint perceived by households and the characteristics of those households who adapt as compared to those who do not adapt.

The results of our investigation of 1 above, are the subject of this chapter. For reasons of economy the analysis of moving behaviour has rested on pre-existing data. The three data bases that were used are described in Appendix B. They include physical and social survey data from the Greater London area, South Hampshire and the West Midlands conurbation. A comparable measure of households' response to their dwellings was available in each survey, whether or not the household intended to move from its present dwelling. Moves which appeared not to be directly related to housing conditions were excluded from the analysis. The data was sufficient to investigate the effects of a number of socio-economic, spatial and physical constraints on the propensity to move. Both univariate and multivariate forms of analysis were undertaken as described in Chapter 5. The data did not permit an analysis of environmental and locational constraints.

Socio-economic constraints

It is to be expected that households will act to reduce their housing disutility subject to a budget constraint; an assumption of disutility reduction rather than utility maximisation. Over time, changes may occur in a household's satisfaction with the services provided by a dwelling as expectations rise, or as the quality of the dwelling and its location deteriorates. This process should result in either a reduction of the relative price that the occupying household is willing to pay, or in a search for a more suitable dwelling. Conversely an increase in the price paid for a dwelling relative to the satisfaction derived should induce changes in the overall pattern of household expenditure or it may lead to a search for alternative cheaper accommodation. While such changes in price relative to quality may not induce an immediate household response, it is reasonable to expect that similar household types will have similar opinions of what constitutes reasonable and unreasonable price ranges for particular types of accommodation. For a given quality of dwelling, or for given satisfaction derived from occupation of that dwelling, one might expect therefore, that the higher the cost the greater the desire or propensity to move.

Our analysis of economic constraint set out to investigate three basic questions: firstly, whether there were significant differences in the incomes of movers and non-movers, secondly, whether there were significant differences in the housing costs of movers and non-movers, and finally, whether there were significant differences in the proportion of income spent on housing between movers and non-movers.

Income is probably the most basic factor affecting housing conditions. Households income sets the ultimate limit on the ability to pay and the ability to move. Housing shortages, inertia and ignorance of opportunities may prevent some households from improving their housing conditions, but income is the primary constraining factor.

The first variable examined was the relationship between the desire to move — as indicated by the number of households wishing to move as a proportion of all households — and head-of-household and household income. This probability of moving, by income level, is shown in Figures 6.1 and 6.2. The income figures used are for take-home pay, i.e. income net of tax and insurance contributions. The distributions for the West Midlands and GLC data show marked similarities, the highest probabilities of moving occurring in the middle income ranges. A comparison of these figures suggests that any household income over and above that earned by the head of household, increases the probability of moving in the lower-middle income range. Rather surprisingly, in both the West Midland and GLC data, the mean level of household income was slightly higher for non-movers than for movers, although not to a significant degree.

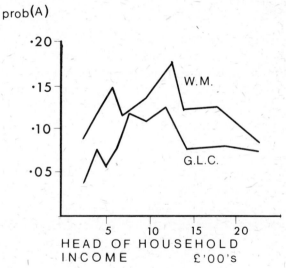

Figure 6.1   Moving and head of household income

Any interpretation of the relationship between the desire to move and income level must take account of the two interacting aspects noted above: the intention to improve housing conditions through moving, and the financial ability to do so. For example the lower-income households generally occupy the cheaper, poorer-quality dwellings. It is to be expected that a high proportion of these households will be dissatisfied with their housing conditions and express an intention to move. However, a

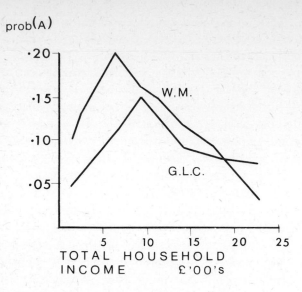

Figure 6.2   Moving and total household income

high desire to move may be masked by the realisation of a low financial ability to do so. On the other hand, the higher-income groups occupy better-quality dwellings and it is to be expected that a lower proportion of these households will be dissatisfied and express an intention to move for housing reasons. However, this proportion wishing to move will be able to do so because of greater financial resources. Figures 6.1 and 6.2 can therefore be interpreted as follows:-

1   The overall probabilities of moving are 'low to average' in the lower income ranges. This may be the result of a high desire to move coupled with a low financial ability to do so.
2   The probabilities of moving are 'average to high' in the medium income ranges. This is probably due to the combination of an average desire to move and an average financial ability to do so.
3   The probabilities of moving are 'average to low' in the higher income ranges. This may be the result of a low desire to move coupled with a high financial ability to move.

The second variable examined was housing costs. Households incur two types of housing cost: the direct costs of occupying a dwelling — rent, rates, mortgage and maintenance expenditure, and indirect costs due to the location of the dwelling — mainly transport costs. It is the first category, direct housing costs, with which we are concerned here. The increase in housing costs incurred by a household as a result of improving its housing conditions by moving or adapting is an approximate indicator of the household's valuation of the new situation compared with the old. We may interpret the difference between the old and new costs as an approximate valuation, made by the household, of the degree of constraint that has been removed. In some cases costs may decrease as a result of a move and if housing conditions have been improved then the household will be better off on both counts. In most cases housing costs will increase with a move, for example when a household moves from private rented to the owner-occupied sector. In this case we can assume that the household values owner occupation as opposed to renting, at least as much as the measured disbenefit.

Housing costs may be unacceptable to a household simply because they too tightly constrain expenditure on other items in the household's budget. In this case the level of housing expenditure cannot reasonably be afforded given the available household income. Alternatively, housing costs may be unacceptable if, in the opinion of a household, the space, services and amenities provided by the dwelling and its location are inadequate relative to the price being paid. Over time, housing costs may become increasingly unacceptable as rents, rates and mortgage payments rise relative to income, as the quality of a dwelling declines relative to its cost, or as the household income available to meet housing costs falls.

The degree to which housing expenditure varies with income and other socio-economic variables has been studied before[1],[2] and the sensitivity of housing expenditure to changes in household income has been examined. Type of tenure also influences decisions concerning housing expenditure, for example the fact that rent payments represent payment for current consumption of housing services, while mortgage repayments are both a form of saving and a hedge against inflation. Moreover, in the owner-occupied sector, mortgage repayments can be a misleading measure of real housing costs since the level of repayment at any point in time is a complex function of the amount borrowed, the duration of the loan, the interest rate, the original price of the dwelling and the date of purchase. It is necessary to recognise that households may actually maximise their mortgage repayments initially, since such outgoings are relatively fixed while household income tends to rise over time. Recent attempts have been made to assess the real cost for owner-occupiers in order to derive a measure which can be meaningfully compared with renters' payments.[3] This is achieved by treating housing as a consumer durable and estimating its real cost by assessing the opportunity cost of the capital invested in the dwelling and adjusting this sum for the capital gains made as a result of the real increase in house prices. This can then be further adjusted for taxation and subsidies to yield a real net annual housing cost.

Our study of housing obsolescence has not been concerned with assessments of the real value of services consumed by households of different incomes as in the studies noted above, but rather with an examination of the effect of actual housing expenditure on a household's moving behaviour. The analysis therefore concentrated on the relationships between actual expenditure, income and the desire to move.

Expenditure on housing in the allocation of disposable income varies widely with household preference, type of household, tenure group and social class. It is to be expected that the acceptability of various levels of payment for housing services is partially a function of the head of household's income or of the total household income. It was anticipated that an analysis of proportional expenditure (i.e. rent or mortgage payments expressed as a proportion of disposable income) would indicate that the greater the housing expenditure in relation to income the greater the financial constraint imposed on the household and the greater the propensity to move, in order to relax that constraint. Our analysis indicated that this simple hypothesis was not valid. The average expenditure on both rents and mortgages were less for moving than non-moving households, as indicated in Tables 6.1 and 6.2.

Table 6.1

Rent as a percentage of income

Survey Population	Greater London		West Midlands		South Hampshire	
	% of heads' income	% of household income	% of heads' income	% of household income	% of heads' income	% of household income
Movers	22·6	20·9	16·9	11·7	24·6	—
Non-movers	29·9	21·5	19·0	12·4	28·3	—
Total	29·0	20·9	18·7	12·3	28·1	—
Sample size	3033	3020	945	831	219	—

While there is no statistically significant difference between the mean values for movers, and standard deviations were high, the fact that the analysis of all three data cases shows the same direction of difference is, in itself, highly indicative that our original hypothesis was too crudely stated. The probability of moving by cost as a proportion of head's income is shown in Figure 6.3. It can be seen that the proportion of households wishing to move in the GLC falls consistently as proportional costs

Table 6.2

Mortgage repayments as a percentage of income

Population	Survey	Greater London		West Midlands		South Hampshire	
		% of heads' income	% of household income	% of heads' income	% of household income	% of heads' income	% of household income
Movers		13·7	13·1	14·8	13·0	14·8	—
Non-movers		17·7	12·8	16·3	12·8	24·5	—
Total		17·5	13·1	16·2	12·8	24·3	—
Sample size		1242	1211	522	485	131	—

increase. The West Midlands and South Hampshire data bases differ from that of the GLC but are similar to each other, with higher moving probabilities in the lower and middle ranges. Overall, Figure 6.3 indicates a slightly inverse relationship between rent as a percentage of income and the probability of moving. While each of the three data bases differs in detail, the highest proportion of movers always occurs in the lowest proportional rent range where rent is less than 10 per cent of the head of household's disposable income. Those seeking local authority accommodation tended to have higher cost ratios than those moving for other reasons, as did those tenants seeking smaller accommodation; those wishing to enter the owner-occupied sector had relatively low proportional costs of from 11 to 20 per cent.

The proportional amount spent on mortgage repayments by probability of moving is also shown in Figure 6.3. A greater desire to move in the

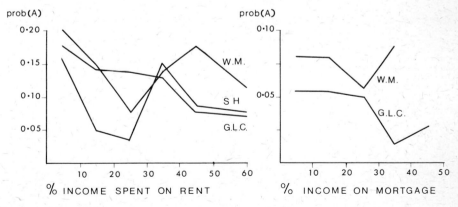

Figure 6.3   Housing costs as percentage of income

lowest and highest ranges of cost is indicated. The U-shaped form of the distribution is similar in both the GLC and West Midlands data. The relatively low values of proportional expenditure on mortgage repayments when compared with rents is to be expected since mortgage repayments are largely determined by the incomes and house prices current at the date of purchase, so the longer the length of stay the lower the proportional mortgage repayment will be. With an average length of stay of around eight years, when owner-occupiers do move then a marked increase in housing expenditure relative to income is to be expected.

These results may be influenced by 'quality' factors. It is to be expected that those households who pay more for their housing will be in receipt of relatively better housing services and may therefore be more satisfied and less likely to move for housing reasons. On the other hand those with low housing expenditure, especially in the private rented sector, are more likely to be occupying dwellings of poor quality, which may increase their probability of moving. A more detailed analysis of proportional housing costs using a crude control for quality of dwelling was undertaken using GLC data. As Table 6.3 shows, when quality was controlled for in this way, the results were much as before, the proportional rent and mortgage costs for non-movers exceeded those for movers.

Table 6.3

Proportional housing costs by house condition (GLC)

Proportional Expenditure	External maintenance			
	Good	Fair	Poor	Unfit
A Movers	25·2	21·7	20·0	23·3
Non-movers	32·0	28·0	29·5	24·9
B Movers	17·2	17·7	16·5	13·9
Non-movers	21·9	21·0	21·4	22·1
C Movers	13·3	13·9	17·4	—
Non-movers	16·8	20·5	17·7	10·1
D Movers	11·9	15·7	4·4	—
Non-movers	12·3	14·7	17·9	6·1

A   Rent as % of head-of-household income
B   Rent as % of total household income
C   Mortgage as % of head-of-household income
D   Mortgage as % of total household income

We may conclude therefore, that within the GLC and West Midland data, proportional housing costs do not appear to exercise an important constraining influence in either the rented or owner-occupied sectors. The economic variables that were available in the data, such as income, rent and mortgage payments, and proportional housing costs, appear to be of limited usefulness in explaining the desire to move. However, households with the largest apparent margin in their ability to afford higher proportional costs had the greatest probability of moving. This suggests that the factors affecting the financial ability to move to better accommodation may be the more important constraints that are acting. This aspect, the effect of economic factors on the ability rather than the desire to move, will be considered in Chapter 7.

The effect of other socio-economic variables on moving behaviour were also investigated, e.g. household type, socio-economic group, age of head of household and tenure. A general description of the effects of these variables has been described in the published accounts of the GLC and West Midlands surveys.[4],[5] They tended to conform to the national pattern.[6] Young families with children have the greatest desire to move. Small adult households and individual adults also exhibit a fairly high mobility. There appeared to be no difference however between the various types of household containing adults of over 60 years of age, all of whom showed a very low desire to move. The age of the head of non-moving households was on average approximately ten years older than that for moving households — an unsurprising finding, given the general greater mobility of younger households.

Finally in this section, we should mention the general effects of tenure on the desire to move. It is clear that the relationship between moving and the tenure of the current dwelling is complex, for different tenures not only imply different levels of security — with respect to both possible eviction and future costs — but also different physical conditions. It is well known for example, that the private rented sector contains the majority of the country's unfit dwellings, as well as offering less security and higher real costs than other tenures. No single measure can allow for these disparate effects on the desire to move. A simple statement of the general position is given in Table 6.4. As might be expected, the privately rented sectors, both furnished and unfurnished, contain the greatest proportion of intending movers, while the owner-occupied sector has the least number of potential movers.

Table 6.4

Proportion of moving households by tenure

Survey	Probability of moving with class of tenure					
	Owner-occupied	Rented from local authority	Rented furnished from private landlord	Rented unfurnished from private landlord	Other tenures	Total cases
South Hampshire	0·17	0·17	0·87	0·30	0·71	729
West Midlands	0·25	0·13	0·15	0·20	0·05	2958
Greater London	0·04	0·10	0·14	0·13	0·17	6591

Spatial constraints

Post-war housing surveys indicate that dwelling size is the most widespread cause of housing dissatisfaction. As a result the relationship between dwelling size and household size, the density of occupation, has become one of the most important indicators of housing conditions. The simple ratio of number of persons to number of rooms is the basis for standards of residential overcrowding. In Britain, the most commonly used standard is the Census definition of 1·5 persons per room while, before 1961, the Census definition was 2·0 persons per room based upon the statutory overcrowding standard[7] first proposed in 1935 and eventually adopted in the 1957 Housing Act. Since this standard was proposed, housing conditions have improved, life styles have changed, occupancy rates have dropped,[8] and expectations concerning the quantity and quality of living space have risen.[9] It has been suggested that, as a result, not only the statutory standard but also the 1961 Census definition may now be inadequate; both the arbitrary basis and the sensitivity of the definition have been questioned.[10] It has been suggested that the age and sex structure of the household and the size and condition of the dwelling may all affect the tolerability of person per room (ppr) ratios.

Two types of potential constraint were examined: the effects of sharing space with other households, and the relationship between the size of dwelling and the size of household, when measured by ppr. With respect to the first constraint, households sharing space had a two to three times greater propensity and desire to move than those households occupying self-contained dwellings. The examination of density of occupation by moving behaviour revealed a consistent pattern in the distribution of ppr values, the mean values and the interquartile ranges of the distributions, the results being remarkably similar in the GLC and West Midlands data. Those households moving for reasons other than size of dwelling also had a considerably higher mean ppr value than the non-moving group, suggesting that spatial constraints are an important contributory factor in cases where the principal reason for moving is not the lack of space. The distribution of occupancy rates and the interquartile ranges of these distributions are shown in Figures 6.4 and 6.5.

The pattern of spatial constraint and its effect on moving behaviour is remarkably similar in the West Midlands and GLC data. From the analyses of the moving data it appears that the acceptable range is less than about 0·9 ppr, the tolerable range is around the 1·0 value, and that values in excess of 1·1 ppr are in the unacceptable category for a high proportion of households.

In the West Midlands survey, two subjective questions were included. These concerned households' opinions of dwelling size and their general satisfaction with their accommodation. This data was not available for comparison in the GLC surveys. From 0·70 ppr upwards, an increasing proportion of households were dissatisfied with the size of their accommodation, but only at 1·3 ppr and higher, was this reflected in expressed dissatisfaction with their accommodation as a whole.

Finally, the accumulative proportion of households wishing to move due primarily to spatial constraint is shown in Figure 6.6. The greatest increase in the proportion of moving households occurs between occupancy rates of 0·8 and 1·2 ppr. An inspection of the results of the various univariate analyses that were undertaken confirms that Census definition of overcrowding — 1·5 ppr — does not correspond with household dissatisfaction as expressed through moving behaviour. Since this definition plays an important role both in the designation of unsatisfactory housing conditions and in the calibration of social indicators such as the Housing Stress Index, we took special interest in this indicator of constraint. The ways in which other variables, in combination with occupancy rate, affect the propensity to move were investigated using a multiple regression technique. The results obtained are discussed later in this chapter.

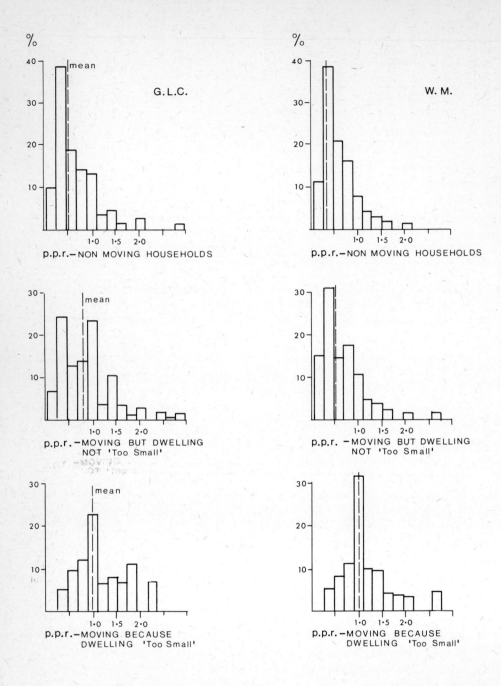

Figure 6.4   Occupancy rate distributions

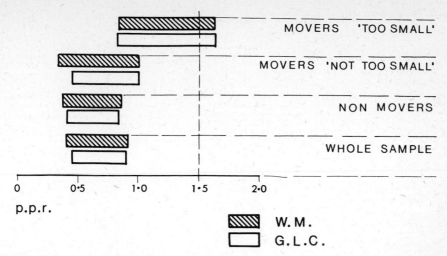

Figure 6.5   ppr — Interquartile ranges

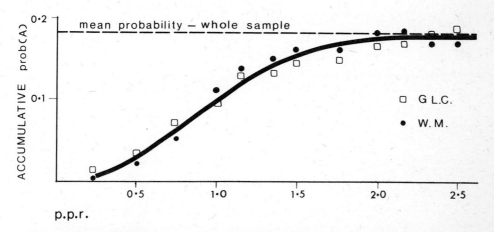

Figure 6.6   Accumulative proportions of households moving because dwelling is 'too small'

Physical constraints

Three types of potential constraint due to physical factors were investigated: the type of dwelling, the facilities offered by the dwelling, and the age and physical condition of the dwelling. Dwellings divided into two distinct classes when their relationship to moving behaviour was investigated. The probability of moving for those households living in maisonettes, converted and purpose-built flats were considerably greater than the probability of those occupying detached, semi-detached or terraced homes, as shown in Table 6.5. Here the influence of dwelling type on the intention to move may have been reinforced by the effects of tenure preferences.

Table 6.5

Effect of dwelling type on the probability of moving (GLC)

	Detached house	Semi-detached	Terraced	Maisonette	Purpose-built flat	Converted flat	Prefab or mobile home	Others
Probability of moving	0·06	0·05	0·08	0·15	0·12	0·14	0·28	0·22
Sample	243	1250	3156	149	848	866	46	79

Facility constraints refer to the presence or absence of certain provisions within dwellings and to their conditions of use, whether they be in the sole use of the household or shared. The measurement of facility constraints is therefore concerned with three possible states – the presence and sole use of a facility, the presence and shared use of a facility and the lack of a facility. The effects of the presence or absence and the sole or shared use of bathroom, wc, basin, sink and cooking facilities on the probability of moving are summarised in Table 6.6. In all cases households having the sole use of each of these facilities had significantly lower probabilities of moving than households sharing facilities. Households sharing facilities had a slightly higher probability of moving than those households lacking such facilities, in all cases.

When we examined the relative importance of individual facilities, it appears that the lack of bath or wc are of equal importance. In each survey the greatest difference in moving intentions between sole and shared use occurred for inside wc's, suggesting that the sharing of this particular facility causes the greatest dissatisfaction. The analysis indicated that the sharing of a bath or bathroom is perceived to be a more serious form of constraint than the sharing of sink, basin or cooking facilities. The availability of piped hot water and full or partial central heading had no effect on the desire to move.

Table 6.6

Effect of sharing or absent facilities
on the intention to move

Facility and survey	Proportion wishing to move			Total cases
	Sole use of facility	Shared use	No facility	
Bathroom (SH)	0·21	0·46	0·28	727
Bath/shower (WM)	0·09	0·27	0·24	2890
Bath/shower (GLC)	0·06	0·14		6373
Inside wc (SH)	0·20	0·50	0·31	729
Inside wc (WM)	0·09	0·31	—	2451
Outside wc (WM)	0·19	0·38	—	505
Sink (WM)	0·11	0·29	0·25	2878
Basin (WM)	0·09	0·26	0·19	2888
Cooking facilities (GLC)	0·09	0·20		6409
All facilities (GLC)	0·06	0·13		6591
Rateable Unit (WM)	0·05	0·14	—	2974

The age and condition of dwellings are two of the traditional variables used in official studies of housing obsolescence. The effects of age and condition on moving intentions are shown in Figures 6.7 and 6.8. In spite of marked differences between each of the three data bases, the overall U-shaped relationship seems to be fairly well established. Taken at face value, Figure 6.7 would suggest that pre-1919 dwellings are the most undesirable, and that post-1944 dwellings are relatively undesirable when compared with dwellings built in the inter-war period. However, the higher proportion of moves from dwellings less than ten years old could be a reflection of relative mobility of the occupants rather than the relative unattractiveness of the dwellings themselves, since it is likely that the more recently built dwellings are occupied by the more mobile younger households. The effects of length of stay may also help to explain the relatively high proportion of intending movers in newer dwellings. If a household has not moved after five years of occupancy then there is a steadily decreasing probability that it will do so the longer it remains in the dwelling. At the other extreme, the increasing probability of moving for those occupying dwellings of fifty years of age and over is presumably due to poorer physical conditions and facilities, together with the higher levels of maintenance cost involved.

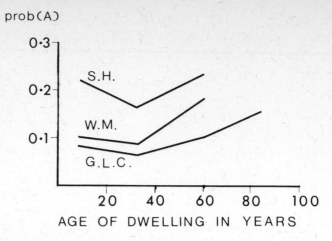

Figure 6.7   Probability of moving by age of dwelling

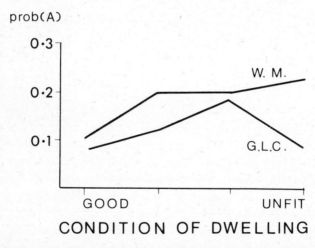

Figure 6.8   Probability of moving by condition of dwelling

The effects of physical condition of the dwelling on the desire to move were investigated both in terms of the 'estimated' fitness of the dwelling and the actions taken under the 1957 Housing Act; the results are shown in Tables 6.7 and 6.8. In the case of the West Midlands data the results were as expected, with significantly higher probabilities of moving for those in 'unfit' as against 'fit' dwellings, and for those in the 'action' as against 'no action' categories under the 1957 Housing Act. In the case of the GLC data the results were less clear, with the lowest probabilities of moving occurring in the 'unfit' and 'good' categories. The low proportion of households moving from unfit dwellings in the GLC may be due to the absence of alternative accommodation and the lower expectations of these households, rather than any positive wish to remain where they are.

Table 6.7

Effect of physical condition on
the probability of moving

Fitness criteria	Condition				Total cases
	Unfit	Poor	Fair	Good	
External maintenance, GLC	0·08	0·17	0·11	0·06	6587
Structural condition, GLC	0·08	0·20	0·12	0·06	6591
Estimated fitness, WM	0·24	0·20	0·20	0·10	2678

Table 6.8

Effect of action under 1957 Housing Act

GLC	No action	Redevelopment proposed	Action under Act proposed	Action planned under Act
Proportion wishing to move	0·08	0·15	0·18	0·21
Sample	5968	208	89	326

WM	No action	Action planned under Part II	Action planned under Part III
Proportion wishing to move	0·10	0·12	0·27
Sample	2344	74	260

Part II of the 1957 Act refers to the local authority's power to close and demolish an individual dwelling, but with no statutory requirement to rehouse the inhabitants. Part III concerns the clearing of areas of housing, with the condition that the authority rehouse those that are dispossessed. These households are likely to be allocated to local authority stock and this probably explains the greater moving response by households who might be affected by Part III action, than those who may be affected by actions taken under Part II.

Given the limitations of the available data, our univariate analysis of simple constraint variables generated a number of interesting results, especially with respect to economic and spatial constraints. Most, if not all, the socio-economic, spatial and physical constraints investigated are inter-correlated, so our next task is an assessment of the effects of combinations of potentially constraining factors on the propensity to move.

Constraint and the propensity to move

The combinational effects of housing constraints were analysed using a standard type of multiple regression program. This type of analysis, which was briefly described in Chapter 5, can include only those cases for which there are values for all of the variables that are to be examined. Cases with missing values for one or more variables must be excluded. As a result the multivariate analysis could only be completed using the West Midlands data, owing to missing values in a high proportion of the economic variables in the other surveys. The dependent variable in our analysis took the value of 1 if the household wished to move and 0 if it did not. The dependent variables were selected as follows: Firstly, we listed those variables which had had a discernible effect on the propensity to move in the univariate analysis of socio-economic, spatial and physical constraints. A few variables were eliminated or combined due to missing data. The list was further reduced on the basis of F-tests carried out in a number of preliminary runs of a stepwise multiple regression analysis. The following ten variables remained:

1 Condition of dwelling
2 Age of dwelling
3 Type of dwelling
4 Annual housing cost (rent or mortgage)
5 Presence or absence of bath or shower
6 Annual income of head of household
7 Age of head of household
8 Occupancy rate (ppr)
9 Tenure
10 Length of stay at present address

Each of these was transformed into a number of binary variables, the scale divisions being selected on the basis of the results of the univariate analysis. The final runs of the multiple regression analysis were carried out separately for the owner-occupied and rented sectors since quite different effects and interactions seemed to be acting in these two sectors.

From the overall pattern of interaction, it was possible to isolate seventeen significant interactions in the rented sectors and eight significant interactions in the owner-occupied sector. These are illustrated in Table 6.9. The regression equation for the rented sector can be written as

$$\hat{Y} = \text{prob}\,(Y = 1) = 0{\cdot}067 + \sum_{i=1}^{i=17} F_i \pm 0{\cdot}333 \qquad (6.1)$$

The R^2 for the regression is $0{\cdot}1840$, and F for the analysis of variance is $5{\cdot}348$ with 32 and 759 degrees of freedom.

The regression equation derived from the analysis of owner-occupiers can be written as:

$$\hat{Y} = \text{prob}\,(Y = 1) = 0{\cdot}063 + \sum_{i=1}^{i=8} F_i \pm 0{\cdot}241 \qquad (6.2)$$

R^2 for the regression is $0{\cdot}0553$ and F for the analysis of variance is $2{\cdot}591$ with 10 and 443 degrees of freedom.

Table 6.9 shows that five of the original ten variables appear most frequently in the interactions. The variable describing the age of dwelling is the most frequent. It is included in six of the seventeen interactions in the rented sectors and in four of the eight interactions in the owner-occupied sector. The occupancy variable is the next most frequent, followed by the variables describing housing cost, age of head and tenure. At the other extreme the variable describing the condition of dwellings is included in none of the interactions in any sector. The effects of the more frequently occurring variables on the propensity to move will now be explained. The values of F_t in the regression equations are listed in Tables 6.10 and 6.11, the regression coefficients and their standard errors are also given for each variable along with the definition and states of the included variables.

The effect of age of rented dwelling in combination with the other variables is interpreted in Figure 6.9 which shows the positive and negative influences on the propensity to move, as the effects of each of the interactive variables are accounted for in turn. For example, the combined effects of age of dwelling and occupancy are shown in column 1. Here we see that the combination of a pre-1919 dwelling with occupancy greater than 1·1 ppr (B) has the most marked positive effect on the intention to move for housing reasons. In column 2 the variable describing the presence or absence of a fixed bath is introduced and the diagram indicates the marginal effect of this variable. Finally, column 6 in Figure 6.9 shows the aggregate effects, both positive and negative, of the six variables on the

111

Table 6.9
Interactions

Rented Sectors

Interactions

	F_1	F_2	F_3	F_4	F_5	F_6	F_7	F_8	F_9	F_{10}	F_{11}	F_{12}	F_{13}	F_{14}	F_{15}	F_{16}	F_{17}
1 Condition of dwelling																	
2 Age of dwelling				X	X	X	X	X	X								
3 Type of dwelling						X						X					
4 Housing costs							X						X			X	X
5 Presence of bath					X					X							
6 Income													X	X	X		
7 Age of head		X						X							X		X
8 Occupancy rate	X			X						X	X	X					
9 Tenure									X		X	X		X		X	
10 Length of stay			X														

Owner-occupiers

Interactions

	F_1	F_2	F_3	F_4	F_5	F_6	F_7	F_8
1 Condition of dwelling								
2 Age of dwelling				X	X	X		X
3 Type of dwelling								
4 Housing costs						X	X	
5 Presence of bath					X			
6 Income							X	
7 Age of head	X	X						
8 Occupancy rate				X				
9 Tenure			X					
10 Length of stay								X

Table 6.10
Regression coefficients of interactions in the owner-occupied sector

	Interactions	Regression coefficient and standard error	F-Value	No. of cases
F_1	Occupancy			
	More than 0·9 ppr	− 0·083 ± 0·037	5·035	80
	0·9 ppr or less	0		374
F_2	Age of household head			
	0–44 years	0		290
	45 and over	− 0·041 ± 0·025	2·641	164
F_3	Length of stay at present address			
	Less than 6 years	0		194
	6 years or more	0·041 ± 0·027	2·346	260
F_4	Age of dwelling and occupancy			
	Dwelling built between 1919 and 1944 occupancy more than 0·9 ppr	0·072 ± 0·062	1·349	27
F_5	Age of dwelling and annual income of household head			
	Dwelling built between 1919 and 1944, income up to £1010	− 0·053 ± 0·032	2·691	112
	Inter-war dwelling, income £1010 to £1336	0·051 ± 0·042	1·468	48
F_6	Age and cost of dwelling			
	Dwelling built before 1919 and costing between £125 and £192 pa	0·111 ± 0·052	4·543	28
	Inter-war dwelling costing between £125 and £192 pa	0·045 ± 0·036	1·554	75
F_7	Cost of dwelling and income of household head			
	Dwelling costs between £125 and £192 pa and income of £1010 to £1336	0·037 ± 0·049	0·558	35
F_8	Length of stay and age of dwelling			
	Stayed 6 years or more and dwelling built before 1919	− 0·050 ± 0·040	1·608	57

Table 6.11
Regression coefficients of interactions in the rented sector

Interactions		Regression coefficient and standard error	F-Value	No. of cases
F_1	Occupancy			
	Less than 0·5 ppr	0		296
	0·5—1·1 ppr	− 0·084 ± 0·045	3·509	380
	Over 1·1 ppr	− 0·083 ± 0·069	1·454	116
F_2	Age of household head			
	Under 25	0		16
	25—44	0·002 ± 0·044	0·001	274
	45 and over	0		502
F_3	Length of stay at present address			
	Less than 6 years	0		206
	6 years or more	0·059 ± 0·030	3·893	586
F_4	Age of dwelling and occupancy			
	Dwelling pre-1919 over 1·1 ppr	0·257 ± 0·152	2·866	30
	Inter-war dwelling 0·5—1·1 ppr	0·029 ± 0·049	0·345	149
	Inter-war dwelling over 1·1 ppr	0·168 ± 0·083	4·115	44
F_5	Age of dwelling and presence of bath or shower			
	Dwelling built before 1919 and no bath or shower	− 0·154 ± 0·070	4·884	131
F_6	Age and type of dwelling			
	Pre-1919: semi-detached	0·214 ± 0·127	2·837	9
	Pre-1919: terrace	0·319 ± 0·073	19·106	163
	Pre-1919: flat etc.	0·266 ± 0·118	5·055	13
	Inter-war: flat etc.	− 0·149 ± 0·113	1·749	10
F_7	Age and cost of dwelling			
	Pre-1919: £53—£78 pa	0·067 ± 0·066	1·021	39
	Pre-1919: over £78 pa	− 0·191 ± 0·102	3·497	25
	Inter-war: over £78 pa	− 0·169 ± 0·050	11·297	139
F_8	Age of dwelling and age of household head			
	Pre-1919: head 65 or over	− 0·116 ± 0·070	2·744	55
	Inter-war: head 45—64	0·123 ± 0·049	6·365	143

Table 6.11 continued

	Interactions	Regression coefficient and standard error	F-Value	No. of cases
F_9	Age of dwelling and tenure			
	Pre-1919: private renters	-0.071 ± 0.059	1·435	
F_{10}	Occupancy and presence of bath or shower			
	0·5–1·1 ppr: no bath or shower	0.256 ± 0.081	10·038	44
	Over 1·1 ppr: no bath or shower	0.150 ± 0.148	1·018	26
F_{11}	Occupancy and tenure			
	0·5–1·1 ppr: private renters	-0.144 ± 0.066	4·801	53
	Over 1·1 ppr: private renters	-0.277 ± 0.116	5·697	13
F_{12}	Occupancy and type of dwelling			
	0·5–1·1 ppr: flats, maisonettes etc.	0.223 ± 0.052	18·007	66
	Over 1·1 ppr: flats, etc.	0.471 ± 0.106	19·649	14
F_{13}	Annual income and annual cost of dwelling			
	Head's income up to £520: cost between £53 and £78	0.048 ± 0.043	1·265	111
F_{14}	Annual income and tenure			
	Income £521–£780: private renters	-0.105 ± 0.081	1·660	24
F_{15}	Annual income and age of household head			
	Income up to £520: 65 and over	-0.072 ± 0.050	2·059	161
	Income £521–£780: 25–44	0.131 ± 0.054	5·841	50
F_{16}	Housing costs and tenure			
	Costs over £78 pa: private renters	0.157 ± 0.072	4·786	49
F_{17}	Housing costs and age of household head			
	Costs £53–78 pa: head 45–64	-0.146 ± 0.049	8·863	103
	Costs over £78 pa: head 25–44	0.111 ± 0.049	5·131	140
	Costs over £78 pa: head 65 and over	0.219 ± 0.069	10·173	47

115

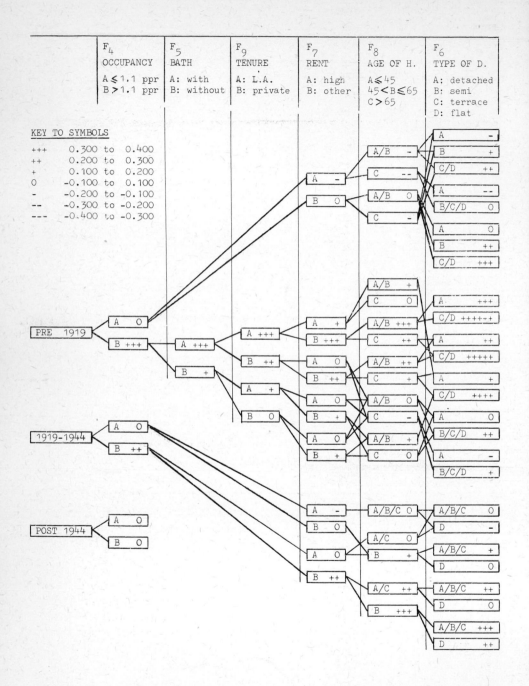

Figure 6.9   Interactions between age of rented dwellings and other variables

propensity to move of households in pre-1919, 1919–44 and post-1944 dwellings. The figure gives a very simplified view of the actual results. Only the relative effects of combinations of variables are described, the actual numbers produced by the multivariate analysis should not be interpreted as directly representing moving probabilities.

Generally, the older the dwelling the greater the likelihood of the occupying household wanting to move. However, this age effect was different for different types of dwelling, e.g. the probability of wanting to move from an old terrace dwelling was approximately 1·4 times that of wanting to move from an old semi-detached dwelling. The occupancy rate of post-war dwellings *per se* had no discernible effect, either positive or negative, on moving intentions. Overcrowding compounded the effects of the age of dwelling. Occupancy rates higher than 1·1 ppr greatly increased the likelihood of wanting to move for those households occupying pre-1919 and inter-war rented dwellings. In the owner-occupied sector the age of dwelling has considerably less effect on the propensity to move. Households with medium incomes and medium mortgage commitments occupying inter-war dwellings appear to be the most likely to move in this sector.

The variable describing the presence or absence of bath, coupled with a high occupancy rate, modified the moving propensities but not to a marked degree. The introduction of the age-of-head variable has a negative effect for those over 65 years of age who were occupying pre-1919 rented dwellings. Finally, the interaction between the age and type of dwelling has a strong positive effect on the propensity to move from pre-1919 dwellings. We may conclude that, for the rented sectors, age of dwelling, in combination with occupancy rate and type of dwelling, has important positive effects on moving propensity. The highest propensity occurred in pre-1919 terraced dwellings with low rent levels, in which the ppr ratio was greater than 1·1 and in which the head of household was less than 65 years old. The lowest propensity occurred in privately rented detached dwellings and inter-war flats with high rent levels, in which the ratio of person per room was less than 1·1 and the head of household was more than 65 years of age.

The interaction of the age of head of household with age of dwelling, income and rent is illustrated in Figure 6.10. The highest moving propensity is apparent in the 25–44 age range for those households with a medium level of income who are paying a high level of rent. The lowest propensity occurs in those households in which the head is over 65 years old with low income, and paying low or medium levels of rent.

The interactive effects of occupancy rate in the rented sectors are summarised in Figure 6.11. An occupancy rate of greater than 1·1 ppr

117

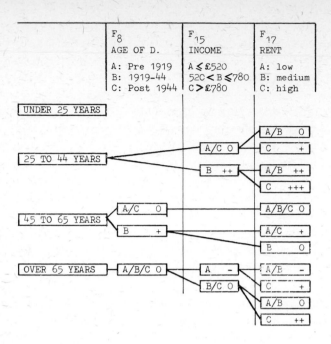

Figure 6.10   Interactions between age of head and other variables in the rented sector

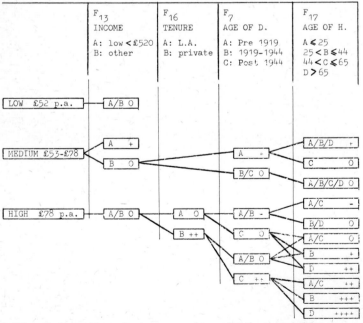

Figure 6.11   Interactions between rent and other variables

generally increased the likelihood that a household will want to move. The highest positive values all occurred in flats in the local authority sector. This is probably due to tenants' knowledge of the importance of overcrowding as grounds for changing local authority dwellings, reflected in the respondents' stated intentions about moving. In the private rented sector, higher occupancy rates appear to be more acceptable to those occupying detached, semi-detached and terraced dwellings than to those households living in flats, while the older the dwelling the greater the effect of overcrowding. The combination of a high occupancy rate of more than 1·1 ppr with a pre-1919 flat lacking a bath, gave rise to the greatest propensity to move in this sector. The lowest propensity to move for households living at more than 1·1 ppr was for those occupying private post-war accommodation other than flats. The relative magnitude of the interactive effects of high occupancy rate with other variables adds weight to the importance of overcrowding as an indicator of generally poor housing conditions.

Cross-tabulations of occupancy rate with each of the interactive variables were examined. These were disaggregated by household and dwelling type, the classification frame being derived from cluster analyses of the GLC and West Midlands data. The most important finding was that households with children in the privately rented sector experienced the greatest spatial constraint. Moreover, in all tenure classes in both the GLC and West Midlands data, it was the households with children that had the greatest probability of moving and that also had higher ppr ratios than other household types. When the reasons for moving were analysed by household type, it was again the households with children who showed the greatest propensity to move due to dissatisfaction with the size of their present accommodation. At the outset of our study it was expected that, since young children of the same sex commonly share bedrooms, the simple unadjusted ppr ratio would overestimate the degree of overcrowding in households with children. Our findings suggest that the opposite is probably the case and that tolerabilities of occupancy rates are lower for households with children than for those without. It would appear that unadjusted ppr ratios are not comparable, as a means of estimating degrees of overcrowding, between households with children and those without. Ideally, the following type of adjustment should be made:

$$C = \frac{V_1(K_1)}{V_2 + V_3/V_4} \quad \text{or} \quad C = \frac{(V_1 + K_2)}{V_2 + V_3/V_4}$$

where C — adjusted ppr ratio
(K) — adjustment constant
V_1 — population in household
V_2 — total number of rooms private to household
V_3 — number of rooms shared with other household
V_4 — number of households sharing shared rooms

K_1 would take the value 1 for households without children and a value greater than 1 for households with children. Similarly, K_2 would take the values 0, or greater than 0, for households without or with children respectively. The value of K would have to be properly calibrated as a result of survey-supported research into households' tolerabilities. The results of our analyses of the GLC and West Midlands data suggest that figures in the order of 1·2 for K_1 and 1 for K_2 may be appropriate.

The interactive effects of rent levels are shown in Figure 6.12. Older households, occupying the more expensive privately rented modern accommodation, displayed a considerably higher propensity to move than young households occupying pre-war local authority accommodation. This result, as in the univariate analysis, is probably due to the close relationship between the ability and the intention to move. Finally, Figure 6.13 illustrates the interactive effects of tenure, i.e. whether the accommodation is privately or publicly rented. In general, renting in the private rather than the public sector had a negative effect on moving propensity, especially for those households who might have been expected to have a low ability to move — those paying low rent for older accommodation at high occupancy levels. There is one exception to this picture. Those households in modern, high-rent, private accommodation with a low occupancy rate have the highest propensity to move. This again probably reflects a high ability to move. It is interesting to note that as with the univariate analysis the effects of rent and tenure are generally more marked in connection with access constraints than with the constraints due to housing conditions alone.

The interpretation of the results of our multivariate analysis of the relationship between housing constraints and the propensity to move is complex. Clearly the effects of the desire to move and the ability to move overlap. Our analyses appear to have uncovered two general circumstances reflected in moving behaviour.

Group 1

Those households for whom high degrees of perceived housing constraint are reflected in a high propensity to move. This is the general circumstance in which a desire to move is coupled with the ability to do so.

120

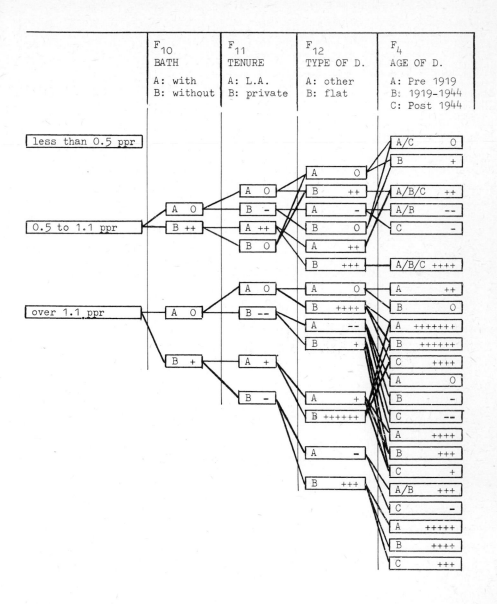

Figure 6.12   Interactions between occupancy rate and other variables in the rented sector

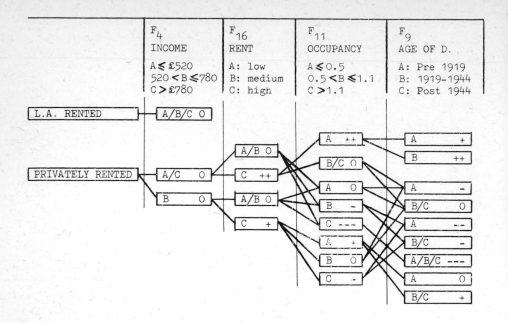

Figure 6.13   Interaction of tenure with other variables

Group 2

Those households for whom we can deduce a *prima facie* case for high constraint but who show a relatively low propensity to move. We believe that this is the circumstance in which a low or negligible ability to move is overriding the desire to move as expressed through a household's stated moving intentions.

We can describe these two groups as follows in the rented sector:

Group 1

Households occupying pre-1919 terraced dwellings or flats
Households occupying old, local authority dwellings
Young and middle-aged households occupying any type of overcrowded dwellings

Group 2

Elderly households occupying overcrowded dwellings in the private sector
Households where the head is over 65 and has a low income
Households occupying overcrowded, old privately rented dwellings with no bath.

Any attempt to define comparable groups in the owner-occupied sector must be more tentative, since fewer significant interactions were obtained and the sample was much smaller than for the rented sector. However, the following general distinctions emerged:

Group 1
Households occupying old dwellings with low housing costs
Households occupying overcrowded dwellings with medium to high income

Group 2
Households occupying overcrowded dwellings with low income
Low-income households with an elderly head
Households occupying old dwellings in which they have remained for a number of years

A given type of housing stock would appear to constrain different types of household in different ways. A particular household type appears to respond differently to the constraints imposed by one type of stock than to similar constraints imposed by another type of stock in a different tenure class, so that in describing the pattern of housing constraint it is desirable to be able to disaggregate households and dwellings into a number of characteristically distinct classes within some classification frame. Five suitable classes of dwelling and five classes of household emerged from the cluster analyses described in Chapter 5. At this five-cluster level, classes of dwelling were discriminated largely by age and type of dwelling, together with the absence or presence of some facilities. Households were discriminated largely by marital status and size. These are illustrated in Table 6.12.

The method of analysis used is hierarchical so the classification may be applied at different levels of aggregation, depending on the requirements of the problem. As the classification becomes disaggregated, the important defining characteristics of stock increase from ones of dwelling type and date of construction, to the number of rooms and the presence or absence of specific facilities. In the case of households, the defining characteristics change from marital status and size to age of head of household and to the distinctions concerning employment. Allowance can also be made in the classification frame, depending on data availability, for those attributes of households and stock that change rather rapidly, e.g. household classes can be disaggregated by level of income, dwelling classes may be sub-divided by price in the case of the owner-occupier or by rent in the other sectors.

Table 6.12

Household and dwelling classification

	Household types	Dwelling types	
Head of household unmarried	H_1 Individual full-time working households H_2 Individual elderly households	D_1 Flats and converted dwellings D_2 Large houses, lacking some facilities (size $>$ 4 rooms)	} Dwellings lacking facilities
Head of household married	H_3 Small families with no children	D_3 Small houses lacking some facilities (size $\leqslant$ 4 rooms)	
	H_4 Large families with children (size $>$ 4) H_5 Small families with children (size $\leqslant$ 4)	D_4 Houses with all facilities built before 1919 D_5 Houses with all facilities built after 1919	} Dwellings with all facilities

Tenure must be included within the classification frame. Table 6.13 gives the overall probability of moving for households in each of fifty housing situation classes for the GLC and West Midlands data. Probability tables of this kind are the starting point for distinctions concerning the different degrees of housing constraint and the different levels of obsolescence that they entail, both for individual types of constraint and for individual housing-situation classes. Two examples will be given. The first describes the effect of different degrees of spatial constraint in the rented sector. The second demonstrates the method of ranking housing situations according to the relative severity of constraint.

The classification of households and dwellings has resulted, by definition, in the distribution of different occupancy rates in various housing situations, particularly in those situations where small (H_3), medium (H_5) and large (H_4) families are matched with small (D) and large (D_2) dwellings. The definition of dwelling classes D_1, D_4 and D_5 does not so limit the values that occupancy rates can take. Table 6.14 shows all the resulting six housing-situation classes ranked from left to right by increasing ppr ratios.

Table 6.13

Aggregate moving probabilities

Survey		Proportion of households wishing to move by housing-situation type									
		Dwelling types: rented sector					Dwelling types: owner-occupiers				
		D_1	D_2	D_3	D_4	D_5	D_1	D_2	D_3	D_4	D_5
GLC											
Household	H_1	·050	·085	·108	·159	·028	·026	0	·034	0	0
types	H_2	·114	·061	·073	·159	·028	·032	·036	·044	0	·025
	H_3	·121	·061	·128	·063	·028	·035	·047	·061	·018	·021
	H_4	·344	·163	·256	·159	·028	·035	·034	·035	·036	·037
	H_5	·188	·063	·243	·019	·028	·085	·063	·023	·041	·037
WM											
Household	H_1	·083	·293	·203	·160	·110	·065	·065	·065	·065	·036
types	H_2	·105	·132	·094	·160	·094	·060	·060	·060	·060	·063
	H_3	·184	·112	·231	·030	·060	·085	:216	·085	·073	·051
	H_4	·156	·273	·457	·160	·076	0	·095	·095	·049	·050
	H_5	·446	·227	·441	·160	·067	·146	·146	·146	·070	·049

Table 6.14

Housing situations ranked by occupancy rate

Proportion wishing to move by housing-situation type in rented sector	ppr value					
	low					high
	H_3D_2	H_5D_2	H_3D_3	H_4D_2	H_5D_3	H_4D_3
	0·4	0·8	0·8	1·0	1·2	2·0
	(max.)	(max.)	(average)	(average)	(average)	(average)
GLC	0·061	0·063	0·128	0·163	0·243	0·256
WM	0·112	0·227	0·231	0·273	0·441	0·457

In all cases the overall probability of wishing to move corresponds to our expectations concerning the effect of increasing occupancy rates. The results of our analysis of spatial constraint suggested that a value of around 1·1 ppr was critical in that, above this value, the proportion of households wishing to move for spatial reasons increased most rapidly. The first three housing-situation classes in Table 6.14 (H_3D_2, H_5D_2, H_3D_3) may therefore be generally described as acceptable and tolerable in respect of the degree of spatial constraint that they imply. A proportion of households in the remaining three classes will consider their occupancy rate as unacceptable and move if they have the ability to do so. The proportion will be greatest in H_4D_3, this class having the highest risk of being considered obsolescent due to lack of space. The class can be disaggregated further by actual household size, dwelling size, age of dwelling and lack of facilities in order that the worst possible combination of conditions be identified.

The second example concerns the relative acceptability of the general conditions in housing-situation classes in the rented sector. The mean probabilities for moving in the GLC and West Midlands data as a whole were 0·1333 and 0·156 respectively in the rented sector, 0·035 and 0·063 respectively in the owner-occupied sector. The overall mean probability of moving in the rented sector was generally exceeded in eight housing-situation classes in the GLC data and in fourteen classes in the West Midlands data. Housing-situation classes can be partitioned into two subsets, those having above, and those having below, the mean moving probability value. The subset with below-mean values (seventeen and eleven housing situations in the GLC and West Midlands data respectively) is composed of a variety of housing situations, all of which may be described as conditions that are 'relatively acceptable'. Some individual households within this subset will, of course, be subject to unacceptable degrees of housing constraint, but within the subset as a whole, relatively acceptable conditions prevail. Individual exceptions to general constraint levels will always be present. The ranking of housing-situation classes within the second subset in which the moving probabilities are in excess of the mean probability, is shown in Figure 6.14.

Moving probabilities are generally lower in the GLC data than in the West Midlands data. This is almost certainly due to differences in the market conditions between the two areas. Figure 6.14 shows that it is the conditions within housing situations H_4D_3, H_5D_3 and H_5D_1, those of large and small families in flats or small dwellings lacking some facilities, that are generally the most unacceptable in both data bases, with the addition of H_4D_1, large families occupying flats, in the GLC area. Although,

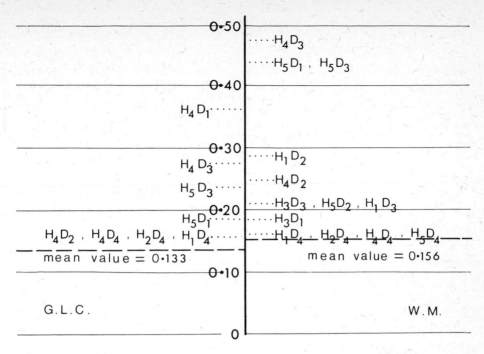

Figure 6.14   Housing situations ranked by moving probabilities

as stated above, some individual households in these relatively unacceptable circumstances may be living in quite acceptable conditions, it is in
these four housing-situation classes, that the risk of obsolescence is the
greatest. As in the first example, given a particular borough or ward, these
situations may be disaggregated further by the introduction of the relevant variables so that the most severely constrained situations are identified.

This approach can be used to identify the thresholds between unacceptable, just-tolerable and acceptable degrees of housing constraint and hence
classify levels of obsolescence. A study of this kind would need to be
supported by a proper survey of housing constraints. Our empirical investigation of housing constraint indicates that the constraining factors
affecting the financial ability to gain access to particular dwelling types
and tenure classes are also of considerable importance. These access constraints are the subject of the next chapter.

127

Notes

[1] J. Vipond and J.B. Walker, 'The Determinants of Housing Expenditure and Owner Occupation', *Bulletin of the Oxford University Institute of Economics and Statistics*, Vol. 34, 1972.

[2] C. Clark and G.T. Jones, *The Demand for Housing*, Working paper no. 11, Centre for Environmental Studies, London 1971.

[3] P. Apps, *An Approach to Modelling Residential Demand*, Paper presented to the Seminar on House Prices and Micro-economics of Housing, London School of Economics, London 1971.

[4] GLC Department of Planning and Transportation, *The Characteristics of London's Households*, Intelligence Unit Research Report, no. 5, 1970.

[5] R.L. Welch, *West Midlands Conurbation Housing Survey 1966*, Housing Survey Reports, no. 6, Department of Environment, HMSO, London 1971.

[6] M. Woolf, *Housing Survey in England and Wales*, Government Social Survey, HMSO, London 1967.

[7] J.B. Cullingworth, *Council Housing, Purposes Procedures and Priorities*, ninth report of the Housing Management Sub-committee of the Central Housing Advisory Committee, HMSO, London 1969.

[8] W.V. Hole and B.A. Pountney, *Trends in Population, Housing and Occupancy Rates 1861–1961*, Department of Environment, HMSO, London 1971.

[9] Parker Morris Report, *Homes for Today and Tomorrow*, Sub-committee of the Central Housing Advisory Committee, HMSO, London 1961.

[10] J. Greve et al., *Homelessness in London*, Scottish Academic Press, Edinburgh 1971.

7 Constraints on the ability to move

The ability to move from one dwelling to another is obviously constrained by the financial resources at a household's disposal in relation to the current price of vacant stock. When households wish to move in order to improve their housing conditions, the amount and type of vacant stock to which they could gain access will itself act as a supply constraint, since households are unlikely to move to dwellings that constrain them more than their current accommodation does. Exceptions may arise when a household is occupying a dwelling which is subject to the decisions of other agents, e.g. landlords evicting tenants, or local authorities condemning unfit stock. It is however, reasonable to assume that 'unforced' moves will not take place unless access to 'better' accommodation is possible.

The distinction between the 'desire' and the 'ability' to move is crucial. The desire to move for housing reasons originates in a household's subjective assessment of its current accommodation and its realisation that, through moving, better housing conditions could be achieved. The ability to move originates in a household's assessment of its financial ability to carry out its desire to move and in the degree to which it might convince the appropriate decision agents of its ability to pay. Access constraints are therefore, those factors which limit or prevent households undertaking a desired move in order to improve their housing conditions. It is through these factors that we can estimate the probability of any household entering a particular dwelling type and tenure class. The broader term, 'access criteria', includes those factors that are taken into account by the various institutions in the housing market when assessing the suitability of households who wish to gain access to a particular dwelling or class of tenure.

The three main housing sectors differ by the types of access constraint they impose. To date, most of the UK housing-market studies have concentrated on the relationship between sets of socio-economic characteristics, especially income and the amount spent on housing. Each sector presents particular difficulties for such analysis. For example, as we have noted earlier, actual housing costs in the owner-occupied sector are not only dependent on the quality and location of the occupied dwelling. The amount spent on mortgage repayments varies with the date at which the mortgage was incurred, the rate of interest charged and the duration of the loan. As a result a number of proxy variables for expenditure have been used in analyses of this sector such as rateable value and imputed rental income.[1],[2] Such analyses both here and in the United States[3],[4] have produced a number of interesting results, especially in estimating the value of the income elasticity of demand for housing. However, it must be said that such studies throw little light on the processes by which households secure dwellings in the owner-occupied sector. An analysis of the rented sectors gives rise to similar problems. For example, in the controlled rented sector there is no necessary relation between ability to pay and rent charged. The analysis of the local authority sector is also complex, firstly because of the administered non-market levels of rent, and secondly because in practice 'local authorities have virtually complete autonomy in the selection of the tenants for their houses'.[5]

We have little precise information about what limits a household's ability to gain access to dwellings both within and between classes of tenure. The results of our investigation of access constraints in the private rented sector, the owner-occupied sector, and the public rented sector will be described in turn. These results are of methodological rather than factual interest. All types of housing constraint are subject to change over time, access constraints being particularly susceptible to rapid change. It should be noted that our empirical results are derived from 1966 data and should not therefore be applied directly to present market circumstances.

Access to dwellings in the private rented sector

In Britain the privately rented sector has shrunk from 90 per cent of the total stock in 1900 to less than 20 per cent in 1970 with evidence to suggest that recently there has been an increase in the rate of reduction. In most of the private rented sector the rate of return is no longer comparable to the returns received on other forms of investment bearing similar risk, because of successive policies of rent regulation and control which have made the provision of rented dwellings a less viable form of investment. The social and economic effects of such policies have been extremely important, the number of dwellings available to rent continues to drop and the supply of new rented dwellings is negligible except in the luxury class. As a consequence, pressure has been increased on the owner-occupied and local authority sectors. In this situation, in which the supply of rented dwellings is shrinking rapidly, and in which demand already exceeds supply, the relationship between quality of dwelling and the ability to pay is likely to become distorted still further. Sitting tenants have a clear advantage while the access of the rest is determined largely by the ability to pay. With the exception of certain ethnic groups and household types who may be discriminated against in particular areas, access in an uncontrolled market is constrained solely by the rent level demanded relative to income. The implications of rent control in the private sector are complex but we would still expect some positive relationship between household income and rent paid. In a situation of complete control the methodology utilised below would be of limited usefulness. However, at the period during which our data was collected, a significant part of the private rented sector was not subject to control and hence the analysis of market processes in this sector could be analysed.

Our analysis of the amount of rent that could be afforded, followed that of other housing expenditure studies.[6] The traditional socio-economic variables were included: income, age of head of household, number of working persons in the household, number of children and social class. Out of our three data bases, only the West Midlands survey was sufficient to support detailed analysis. In this survey a large number of renters indicated that their rent was controlled. These households were omitted from the analysis, to yield a truer measure of the ability to pay. As a result the analysis rests on a much reduced subsample of the original data.

The data used in the analysis gave rise to three other difficulties. Firstly, the West Midlands survey had peculiar tenure classifications. It is stated that a good many households classified as 'other' would on the Census definition be unfurnished or furnished renters. Because of this ambiguity two analyses were attempted: the first (series 1), which included furnished and unfurnished renters as defined in the survey, the second (series 2), which included those households in the 'other' category of the rented sector.

The second problem arises since rents were recorded net of estimated benefits. It is not known what differential bias this might have introduced, but it is safe to assume that the estimates are to some degree biased downwards. Finally, rents were recorded in interval scales and the distribution of rent within these intervals is not known. The midpoint of the range had to be used. An examination of the Family Expenditure Survey (1966–70) indicated that mean income, by income group in that survey, varied unsystematically around — but always close to — the midpoint. We have no reason to believe that any other estimate of heads' income — taking, for example, the upper or lower quartiles — would yield more reliable results than the midpoint approach.

A series of multiple regressions were carried out with this data. The relevant sample taken was for those households who had moved in the year prior to the date of the survey. It is recognised that some changes may have occurred in household characteristics since moving, but by taking only those who had moved during the previous year it was hoped that these changes would be minimal. The data was transformed so that the mean annual rent per income group could define the dependent variable. The selection of independent variables was made *a priori* and on the basis of previous demand studies. For the analysis of both series (1) and (2) the following variables were defined:

Age	— Age of head of household	(continuous)
Income	— Income of head of household	(continuous)
Wrkrs	— Number of working persons	(continuous)
Child	— Number of children ($<$ 16 years)	(continuous)
Dum 1	— Social class of head (I)	(binary)
Dum 2	— Social class of head (II)	(binary)
Dum 3	— Social class of head (III)	(binary)

When the values of Dum 1 to Dum 3 are zero, the function indicates the relationship between the independent and dependent variables for households whose head is social class IV or is 'not economically active'.

Stepwise multiple regressions were performed on data series (1) and (2) and double-log transformations were computed. Both the linear and log-linear relationships were reduced to a more manageable form by the exclusion of non-significant variables. In all cases the number-of-children variable was not significant. All the analyses revealed the expected significant and positive effect of income on the amount of rents paid by households, and the positive effect of being in social class I or II. A negative relationship was yielded with respect to age of head. The analysis indicated an income elasticity of demand with respect to current income of about 0·5. The reduced form of the unlogged regression equation is given below:

Annual Rent

$$R_1 = 61{\cdot}5716 - 0{\cdot}03116^{**} (\text{Age}) + 0{\cdot}0881^{**} (\text{Income}) + 19{\cdot}9829^{*} (\text{Dum 1}) +$$
$$7{\cdot}5364 (\text{Dum 2}) + 1{\cdot}6125 (\text{Dum 3}) + 0{\cdot}6233 (\text{Child}) - 1{\cdot}5083 (\text{Wrkrs})$$

$$R^2 = 0{\cdot}7505 \qquad \left.\begin{array}{l} ** \text{ significant at } \cdot01 \\ * \;\; \text{significant at } \cdot05 \end{array}\right\} \text{ using } F\text{-test} \qquad (7.1)$$

Access to dwellings in the owner-occupied sector

In the owner-occupied sector the probability of access is determined primarily by the decision of relevant credit institutions to provide the purchasing finance. Surprisingly little is known of the precise nature of the decision making process in this respect. However, analytically it may be separated into two aspects: firstly, whether a mortgage will be granted or not, and secondly, if a mortgage is granted, the amount of debt a household will be allowed to incur. The factors constraining households from access to the owner-occupied sector are primarily income, wealth, occupational status and relative house prices. Taking the income variable first, obviously the higher the income the greater the command over credit and the more effectively the household can compete. Since the purchase of a dwelling by mortgage involves a long-term commitment, not only the current income, but also income stability and the employment prospects of the applicant are important. We would expect that the higher the social class of the household the greater the likelihood of receiving a mortgage since the greater the stability and knowledge of the path of future earnings. Since no permanent income data were available for our analysis, we attempted to offset the bias introduced by the use of current income in the analysis by controlling for life cycle/family size and social class factors which may correct the income variable for some of the influences which permanent income represents.

Age adversely affects the ability of a household to gain access to the owner-occupied sector. The older the head of the household the less time is available for any credit to be repaid. Previous owner-occupiers may have a far greater probability of gaining mortgage finance since they will generally have a greater deposit available due to the capital gains made from the sale of their previous dwelling and will also be more knowledgeable about the requirements and procedures of the mortgage institutions. Simply being previous owner-occupiers, irrespective of deposit, may increase this likelihood since the lending institutions are disposed towards those households known to be 'safe' risks. Finally, since credit institutions compete for funds in the investment market, the amount lent and the rate of interest charged to borrowers is normally subject to the fluctuations of that market, and access constraints will themselves fluctuate accordingly.

Our twofold approach to access — analysing both the probability of receiving a mortgage and the amount received — was adopted for three reasons: firstly, because it is not known *a priori* whether high probabilities of obtaining a mortgage are associated with high mortgage advances; secondly, it seemed unwise to assume that all potential households have at least some ability to incur debt and therefore have some possibility of entering the bidding process. Anecdotal evidence suggests that some households who could 'objectively' afford dwellings cannot secure a mortgage, e.g. households with high current incomes but uncertain future earning prospects. Thirdly, adjustments and alterations to two-stage criteria gives extra flexibility in allowing for policy changes. For instance, it is likely that a policy designed to extend mortgages to groups currently excluded from owner occupation will be quite different from a policy which simply seeks to increase the amount current mortgagees can receive.

Two further variables were added to the socio-economic variables used in the analysis of the private rented sector — the size of the deposit available and the previous tenure of the applicant.

Dep — Amount of deposit   (continuous)
Ten — Households previously in owner-occupied
          sector   (binary)

In order to calibrate an access function a sample of those who had moved and who had or had not received mortgages during a one-year period was selected. A binary dependent variable was defined which took the value 1 when a mortgage had been received, 0 when it had not. Here we are unable to differentiate between those who gained access, those who wished to and could not, and those who did not wish to but who could have gained access, and those who did not wish to and could not have gained access. We could only distinguish between those who did and those who did not enter the sector during the period; so the conditional probabilities generated by the regression, if used in a predictive way, will only serve to display the likelihood of access, not that of wishing to and attempting to gain access.

Table 7.1 shows the results of our analysis for owner occupiers, including a variable for total household income (Totinc). Equations (1) and (2) in Table 7.1 indicate that the likelihood of access to mortgate credit is positively related to income (of either type) and negatively related to the age and number of children in the household. However, the variable for previous occupancy in the sector has a particularly marked effect increasing the likelihood of access to credit by over 50 percentage points. Equations (1) and (2) also indicate that, whether for permanent income or other reasons, households in social class I have a significantly greater likelihood of access to mortgage credit than other households with identical characteristics.

Heads income is of particular importance in explaining the amount of mortgage received — equations (3) and (4) in Table 7.1 — although the

Table 7.1

Access in the owner-occupied sector — results of regression analysis

Dependent variables	Constant	Log Income	Log Totinc	Log Wrkrs	Log Child	Log Age	Log Dum 1	Log Dum 2	Log Dum 3	Log Ten_{00}	Log Dep	R^2	Sample
(1) P_{MORG}	-1·04293	*** 0·62917 (0·16767)	Excluded	-0·05768 (0·19491)	** -0·30786 (0·13192)	* -0·32666 (0·24602)	* 0·20897 (0·10288)	0·03414 (0·07892)	(X)	*** -0·56238 (0·08229)	Excluded	0·39732	168
(2) P_{MORG}	-0·59188	Excluded	*** 0·59725 (0·20750)	* -0·52979 (0·24979)	*** -0·35012 (0·13328)	* -0·58037 (0·25153)	*** 0·25958 (0·12450)	0·07732 (0·09949)	0·00877 (0·08240)	*** -0·57404 (0·08239)	Excluded	0·41352	159
(3) Log AMNT	1·15476	*** 0·85155 (0·30429)	Excluded	-0·07666 (0·20718)	* -0·21827 (0·15729)	-0·44337 (0·29464)	** 0·40272 (0·15301)	** 0·29407 (0·12456)	** 0·29669 (0·11970)	*** 0·18567 (0·06572)	(X)	0·56001	52
(4) Log AMNT	2·88866	Excluded	0·31859 (0·32522)	-0·28833 (0·30739)	-0·16421 (0·19683)	-0·56482 (0·34229)	*** 0·58418 (0·15812)	*** 0·39836 (0·13489)	*** 0·39060 (0·13491)	** -0·18668 (0·07483)	-0·02482 (0·08247)	0·48657	49

KEY

Standard errors are given in brackets.

*** = sig at 0·005 level   ** = sig at 0·010 level   * = sig at 0·100 level   (Using 't' test)

(X) indicates that the variable failed the 'floor' significance test for introduction into the equation.

Table 7.2

Access in the local authority sector — results of regression analysis

Dependent variables	Constant	Log Income	Log Totinc	Log Wrkrs	Log Child	Log Age	Log Dum 1	Log Dum 2	Log Dum 3	Log Ten_{LA}	Log Ten_{PR}	R^2	Sample
(5) P_{LA}	-0·54563	* -0·25198 (0·16328)	Excluded	0·05863 (0·17214)	0·11925 (0·12312)	*** 0·84773 (0·21862)	-0·06932 (0·11150)	-0·02057 (0·09120)	0·03933 (0·07698)	*** 0·73990 (0·08136)	*** 0·18715 (0·06669)	0·52025	178
(6) P_{LA}	-0·80571	Excluded	-0·20394 (0·17391)	* 0·31115 (0·21488)	0·12239 (0·12428)	*** 0·91470 (0·22615)	-0·05448 (0·11021)	-0·2728 (0·08965)	0·04137 (0·07470)	*** 0·77785 (0·08198)	*** 0·20745 (0·06923)	0·53504	169

KEY

Standard errors are given in brackets.

*** = sig at 0·005 level   ** = sig at 0·010 level   * = sig at 0·100 level   (Using 't' test)

consistent significance of the social class variables suggest that social classes I to III are highly favoured in the credit allocation process, relative to other social classes. This is particularly true of social class one. The effect of being a previous owner occupier also increases significantly the size of the mortgage received. The deposit variable is insignificant although its negative sign would indicate that generally speaking the higher the deposit the less the mortgage received — and, presumably required.

Access to dwellings in the local authority sector

The local authority sector is an administered market, subject to legislative control. Access to the local authority sector is not determined therefore, by 'usual' economic criteria. In fact, since local authority housing provision is in many ways a welfare service, those factors which aid a household in competing in the two private sectors are likely to reduce that household's chances of being allocated to dwellings in the public sector. For example, on the reasonable assumption that the lower the income of an applicant the greater the need, we would expect that the higher the income of an applicant the less his chance of receiving local authority accommodation. We might therefore expect the effect of social class to be the reverse of that encountered in our analysis of the owner-occupied sector above. We would also expect the age of head to positively effect the likelihood of entry on the grounds that the greater the age of the applicant the lower his ability to command the housing resources of other sectors and the more likely he is to be in need. Of the two non-public sectors, we would expect that those households in the private rented sector were more likely to gain access to the public sector than were owner-occupiers. This is because private rented dwellings are in general of lower quality than in other sectors, households in this sector having less security of tenure, and because the short supply of rented dwellings makes movement within that sector difficult. In addition, the redevelopment and sale for owner-occupation of much of the private rented sector has made the local authority sector the only alternative for many households who are currently renting. It is possible that many families occupying local authority accommodation have higher incomes than those in the private sector, but here we are discussing initial access to the sector, not the effect of changes in income once access has been gained.

The growth of the local authority sector has been partly a response to the decline of the private sector. If access to the local authority sector is in general determined by the perceived degree of need, while access to the

136

rented sector is mainly based on the consumers' ability to pay, then it would seem that unless the function of the local authority sector changes, it could not take over the role of the private rented sector completely. Needs are assessed through a number of factors: the accumulation of welfare points, the position on the waiting list, the accidents of redevelopment and rehousing, and residence requirements. The effect of these factors on access constraints vary with area, according to the particular housing need and the accommodation shortages in that area. Once entry is achieved, the tenant obtains security of tenure, including the opportunity to exchange accommodation if the head of household finds he must move.

The results of the log transforms for the local authority sector are contained in Table 7.2 above and are dominated by the effects of the age of head of household and the previous tenure of the applicant, the quantitative effect of being previously a local authority tenant being particularly marked. The income of the head of household is of negative significance, while that for total household income is not significant. The only other variable to achieve significance is Wrkrs in equation (6), which given that its sign conflicts with that of Totinc suggests that heads income is the truly important variable. None of the introduced social class variables attain significance, which may indicate that current income is of more importance than permament income in the analysis.

In drawing general conclusions from the above analyses it must be remembered that firstly, the data were drawn from one area of the country — the West Midlands — and that secondly, a number of modifications to this data had to be carried out before it became amenable to the method of analysis used. Moreover, the data was for 1966 and quantitative interpretations of our results for current conditions should not be made. However, the method of analysis is — we believe — of particular importance in the context of political decisions concerning housing mobility and obsolescence. Through studies of this kind we can calibrate the various criteria and decision rules that operate in the housing markets. Moreover when these rules are applied to populations of households in particular areas, we can identify the proportion and type of households who are unlikely to be able to improve their housing conditions by moving, either within or between the main housing sectors. Given sufficiently accurate estimates, we can also extrapolate the possible effects of different housing policies on the workings of the housing market.

Notes

[1] J. Vipond and J.B. Walker, 'The determinants of housing expenditure and owner occupation', *Bulletin of the Oxford University Institute of Economics and Statistics,* vol. 34, no. 2, 1972.

[2] C. Clark and G.T. Jones, 'The Demand for Housing', University Working Paper no. 11, Centre for Environmental Studies, London 1971.

[3] R.F. Muth, 'The Demand for Non-farm Housing', in A.C. Harberger (ed.) *The Demand for Durable Goods,* Chicago University Press, 1960.

[4] M.G. Reid, *Housing and Income,* Chicago University Press, 1962.

[5] J.B. Cullingworth, *Council Housing; Purposes, Procedures and Priorities,* Ninth Report of the Housing Management Sub-Committee of the Central Housing Advisory Committee, 1969.

[6] See notes 1, 2, 3 and 4 above.

8   Housing constraint and adapting behaviour

While moving home is the most common way in which households improve their residential conditions, owner-occupiers have the additional opportunity of adapting and modernising their dwellings in order to achieve improvements in their housing conditions. To assist our study of obsolescence, a small survey of some 600 owner-occupiers was undertaken, two-thirds of whom were 'known' to have actively considered adapting their home within the last two years. The purpose of the survey was to discover the degree to which the adaptions and alterations that had been undertaken were made in response to housing constraint. The survey was designed to identify the characteristics of those households that had adapted as opposed to those who had not, to identify the characteristics of the dwellings that were adapted relative to those that were not, and to discover the general types and variety of adaptions and alterations made.

A survey of adaptors

The addresses of those households that have converted or are in the process of converting their dwellings, may be drawn from local authority registers of applications made in accordance with the requirements of the National Building Regulations. These Regulations do not apply to the twelve inner London boroughs, but similar records of conversions and improvements are kept in the offices of the District Surveyors. Three main criteria were used in the selection of study areas. Firstly, the sample was to represent the different characteristics of inner London, suburban London and non-conurbation housing. Secondly, it was to represent a cross-section of structural types of dwelling, and finally, it was to include a variety of ages of dwelling. Four local authority areas in southern England were selected for the survey: the London Boroughs of Camden, Ealing and Richmond; and the Urban District of Winchester.

Four hundred complete interviews of known adaptors and 200 interviews of 'control' households were planned. A random sample of addresses of 'adaptors' was selected for each of the four areas. A random-route approach was designed to select a control sample of 50 households in each area. A total of 573 full interviews were actually achieved, of which 346 were adaptors. Only 73 per cent of the sample of 'known adaptors' had already adapted at the time of interview. However, within the control sample, a surprisingly high proportion of 41 per cent had adapted, bringing the average percentage of adaptors within the total sample to exactly 60 per cent.

Simple tabulations were performed to discover the characteristics of the sample and to describe the range of adaptions, improvements and conversions that had been undertaken. This description of the data was followed by an analysis of the factors that influence the probability of adaption. A statistical package, the Statistical Package for the Social Sciences was used to produce the tabulations and to perform the analyses.

The characteristics of the housing stock and households in the survey sample were examined, together with the types of adaption made. Most of the adapted dwellings in the sample were built before 1919. Few post-war dwellings had been adapted or improved. The dwellings that had been adapted were slightly larger than those that had not been adapted. The mean number of rooms per dwelling for the whole sample was 6·3 rooms while the mean number of rooms for the adapting sample was 6·4 rooms, and for the non-adapting sample, 6·1 rooms. Those households who had moved within three years of the interview date were asked to give the price of their dwelling at the time of purchase. For the whole sample, the mean price was £10,198. For the adapted dwellings the mean price was £9149, and for the dwellings that were not adapted the mean price was £12,482. It can be seen that those dwellings that were adapted were less expensive when purchased than those that were not adapted. These characteristics of adapted and non-adapted dwellings are summarised in Tables 8.1, 8.2 and 8.3. Figure 8.1 gives the distribution of dwellings by type according to whether they were adapted or not.

Table 8.1

Adapted dwellings by age

Date of construction	% of adapted	% of non-adapted	% of all dwellings
Before 1919	52	44	50
1920–39	33	35	34
1940–73	12	17	14
Sample size	100%	100%	100%
	346	227	573

140

Table 8.2

Adapted dwellings by size

Number of rooms	% of adapted	% of non-adapted	% of all dwellings
1–2	0	0·5	0·2
3–4	7	10	8
5–6	54	60	56
7+	39	29	35
Number of bedrooms			
1–2	20	26	22
3–4	70	68	69
5+	10	6	8
Sample size	346	227	573

Table 8.3

Adapted dwellings by price and area

Price £'000	% of adapted dwellings					% of all dwellings				
	Total	Camden	Richmond	Enfield	Winchester	Total	Camden	Richmond	Enfield	Winchester
3–5	8	0	5	20	8	5	0	3	14	6
5–7	18	15	22	27	11	17	13	27	21	11
7–9	16	22	22	10	11	13	15	17	7	15
9–12	14	17	11	7	16	17	18	23	12	17
12–15	14	15	0	10	24	17	23	3	12	21
15–20	10	15	5	7	8	10	12	7	9	8
20–25	0	0	0	0	0	2	3	0	5	0
25+	5	10	0	3	3	5	12	0	2	2
Don't know	16	5	33	17	19	14	3	20	17	17
Sample size (no.)	125	40	18	30	37	181	60	30	92	47

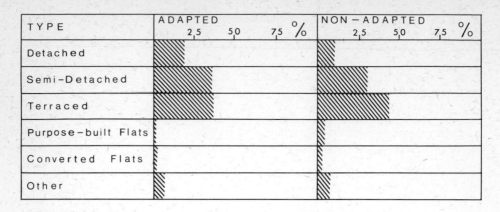

TYPE	ADAPTED 2,5 5,0 7,5 %			NON – ADAPTED 2,5 5,0 7,5 %		
Detached						
Semi–Detached						
Terraced						
Purpose–built Flats						
Converted Flats						
Other						

Figure 8.1　Distribution of adapted and non-adapted dwellings by type

The 'adapting' households in the sample were also proportionally larger than those households who had not adapted. There was a high proportion of five or more person households among the adaptors and a correspondingly high proportion of one- or two-person households among the non-adaptors. The majority of non-adaptors had no children, whereas over half the adaptors had one or more children. The typical profile of the adapting household that emerges is one of a stable family household, with a high proportion of male heads of household, that are married, of working age (20–64) and in full-time employment. This contrasts with the non-adapting household which was characterised, in comparison, by a greater number of single, widowed or divorced heads of household, who were older and, in many cases, retired. Over three-quarters of adapting households had lived at their present address for less than ten years, most having been at their present address for less than three years. In contrast a significant proportion of non-adaptors had lived at their present address for more than eleven years and few had occupied their present dwelling for less than three years. Thus, adapting households would appear to be more mobile than non-adapting households.

A great variety of types of adaptions and improvement had been undertaken. They range from minor repairs, to substantial modernisation and structural alterations to the dwelling. Four main classes of adaption were distinguished in the questionnaire:

1　External and structural adaption
2　The addition of living space by using available space within the existing fabric

142

3   The addition of living space by building additional rooms and extensions
4   Modernisations and improvements

Modernisations, improvements and repairs were the most frequent types
of adaptions undertaken. The addition of space, by building a new room
onto an existing dwelling or by converting unused space, was a major
secondary type of adaption undertaken. Half the adapting households
modernised their kitchen, or installed central heating or electrically re-
wired the dwelling, and over a quarter of the households built a bathroom
and installed an internal wc as part of their adaption. The most common
types of adaption undertaken are illustrated in Figure 8.2.

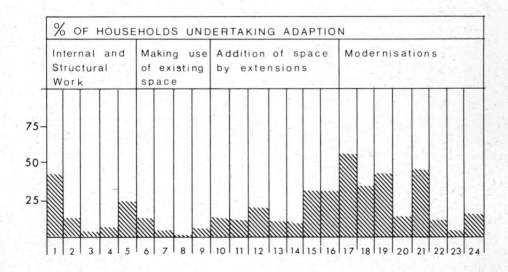

Figure 8.2   Types of adaption undertaken

In order to achieve comparability with our analysis of constraint through moving behaviour, we first analysed the adapting/non-adapting decision with respect to potential constraints considered singly; this was followed by multivariate analysis. As in Chapter 6, we considered the potential constraints under the heads of socio-economic, spatial and physical constraints.

Socio-economic constraints

The process of adaption can be considered as an attempt to reduce any imbalance between the services desired by households and those currently yielded by the dwelling. It is generally considered that many owner-occupiers regard their dwelling as a form of investment. Those adaptions and improvements that increase the market value of a dwelling, also increase the potential capital gain in the future and our results showed that over one-quarter of households adapting their dwellings did so to increase the value of their property. However, this was the most important reason for adapting for only 3 per cent of the adapting sample. While no other economic considerations were apparent through the expressed reasons for adapting, the results of our univariate analysis of socio-economic constraint suggest that in many cases they are important reasons for non-adaption.

One of the most marked differences between adaptors and non-adaptors is that, among adaptors, there are more heads of household from professional social groups and fewer heads of household from the semi-skilled group (SEG IV). Of those who adapt, half are in SEG I, a quarter in SEG II, and a decreasing number in SEG's III and SEG IV. A difference between the income of the adaptors and the non-adaptors was also apparent. The mean weekly income of the adaptors (head of household) was £45·5 compared with a mean weekly income for non-adaptors of £33·5, a statistically significant difference of £10 per week. Not only is there a substantial income difference between those households that do adapt and those that do not, but there are very few adapting households in the lowest income groups. Among adaptors, only thirty households had incomes below £30 per week, whereas 194 households had incomes over £30 per week. The effects of social-economic class and income are summarised in Tables 8.4 and 8.5.

As noted earlier, prices paid by recent movers for dwellings subsequently adapted by them, were less, on average, than those for dwellings that remained unadapted. Some 36 per cent of all adaptions undertaken in the sample cost over £2000, and more than 60 per cent cost over £1000. Our analysis shows that many higher-income households decided to purchase a less expensive house and adapt it to their requirements rather than purchase a higher-standard dwelling for a higher price. A number of households in the lowest income group (less than £30) also undertook high-cost adaptions. The group of households with incomes between £50 and £60 moderate their costs, and less than half of them undertake adaptions costing over £1000. It would appear that once the decision to adapt is taken, income is no longer the single overriding factor affecting expenditure on adaption. Figure 8.3 shows the percentage of households within each income group who undertake adaptions in each cost category.

Table 8.4

Socio-economic class of adaptors and non-adaptors

SEG	% of adaptors	% of non-adaptors	% of movers	% of all households
Professional (I)	50	41	51	47
Managerial (II)	28	33	21	29
Skilled (III)	18	14	19	16
Semi-skilled (IV)	4	12	9	7
Sample size	346	227	57	573

Table 8.5

Head of household income for adaptors and non-adaptors

Weekly income	% of adaptors	% of non-adaptors	% of movers	% of all households
0–£10	3	4	2	3
£10–£19.99	1	4		2
£20–£29.99	5	10	7	7
£30–£39.99	9	8	5	8
£40–£49.99	11	9	3	10
£50–£59.99	11	10	5	10
£60–£69.99	7	6	7	7
£70–£119.99	9	6	14	8
£120 over	9	4	10	7
Don't know/ Won't say	35	40	46	37
Sample size	346	227	57	573

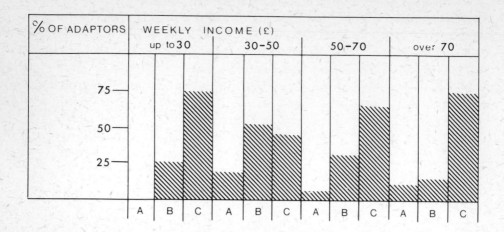

Figure 8.3   Household income and adaption costs

In our sample, only 2 per cent of adapting households received improvement grants. Some 70 per cent of the adaptions costing up to £250 were paid for from household savings. Many of these adaptions received improvements grants from the local authority to meet up to half the cost. From £2000 upwards, the proportion of adaptions that are paid for from savings remains fairly constant, but the proportion of payments from bank loans steadily increased. Generally, once the cost of adaption reached £1000, most households used two or more sources of finance to pay for the adaption. In the cost category of £2000 plus, over half the households used a bank loan to pay for some or all of the cost. Table 8.6 details the ways in which adaptions were financed.

Table 8.6

Cost of adaption by source of payment

Source of payment	Cost of adaption						
	Up to £125	£126–250	£251–500	£501–1000	£1001–1500	£1501–2000	£2000+
Savings	93%	46%	88%	69%	61%	64%	65%
Improvement grant	–	31%	6%	4%	28%	10%	42%
Bank loan	–	–	20%	33%	28%	39%	51%
Local authority loan	–	–	3%	2%	–	3%	11%
Other	–	–	–	2%	11%	13%	5%
Sample size	15	13	35	46	46	31	103

146

Our survey discovered that a remarkably high proportion of households reduced the cash outlay on adaption by undertaking themselves some or all of the work involved, as illustrated in Figure 8.4. Table 8.7 gives details of the types of adaption undertaken by households themselves. The most common type of self-help concerned kitchen improvements. 51 per cent of households who modernised their kitchen, undertook some or all of the work themselves.

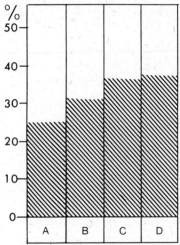

Figure 8.4   Proportion of households undertaking adaption work themselves

Spatial constraints

One of the purposes of the survey was to investigate the reasons why dwellings had been adapted. The most commonly expressed was the need for more living space. In answer to an open-ended question concerning the reason for adapting, some 28 per cent of the households interviewed replied to increase living space. This was also the response given by 25 per cent of the households as the most important reason for adapting their dwelling. Moreover, many adapting households had also moved from their previous dwelling because they needed larger accommodation. It would appear that the spatial constraints imposed by the dwelling are as important an originator of adapting behaviour as they were of moving behaviour. Our examination of occupancy rate by adapting behaviour in the owner-occupied sector confirms the general trend of the findings described in Chapter 6 but with lower occupancy rates generally.

Table 8.7

Households undertaking adaption work themselves

Type of adaption	No. of adaptions	No. of households	No. of households who undertook work				Households as % of adaptions
			Amount of work undertaken				
			All	Some	Very little	Don't know	
External repairs	136	40	21	12	5	2	29
Divided dwelling	37	8	5	3	–	–	21
Combined dwelling	8	1	1	–	–	–	12
Increased no. of rooms	22	7	4	2	1	–	32
Decreased no. of rooms	85	36	24	9	2	1	42
Attic into use	37	15	7	6	2	–	42
Basement into use	15	4	1	1	2	–	27
Garage into use	8	2	–	1	1	–	25
Other into use							
Add bedroom	49	17	5	7	4	1	35
Add living room	41	10	1	4	3	2	24
Add kitchen	72	34	19	10	2	2	47
Add sun room	34	14	4	3	5	2	41
Add other	31	10	1	4	3	2	32
Built bathroom	103	35	14	10	9	2	34
Built internal wc	104	32	14	7	10	1	31
Modernise kitchen	195	100	55	28	11	2	51
Modernise bathroom	113	52	31	11	7	3	46
Install central heating	144	36	19	8	5	4	25
Built a garage	43	22	5	11	2	2	51
Rewire	155	49	27	14	4	3	32
Plumbing	36	8	4	3	1	–	22
Floor and ceiling	10	3	1	2	–	–	30
Others	54	16	11	4	1	–	30

Changing household circumstances and standards of living can affect the tolerability of occupancy densities. In our sample, the average occupancy rate was low. The mean person per room (ppr) ratio for the whole sample was 0·54. Those adaptors who had added a room, or in some way increased the living space of their accommodation were separated from those who had only modernised or improved their accommodation, and the mean ppr ratios prior to adaption were calculated. Before adaption, the mean ppr ratio of the group that added a room was 0·68 and the addition of a room reduced this ratio, on average, to 0·56. The mean ppr ratio of the group who did not add a room was 0·57. These results are shown in Table 8.8 and in Figure 8.5. It may be concluded that when households are living at occupancy rates of about 0·7, rates that are generally considered to give very satisfactory living conditions, they still perceive sufficient spatial constraint to warrant expenditure on extensions and conversions.

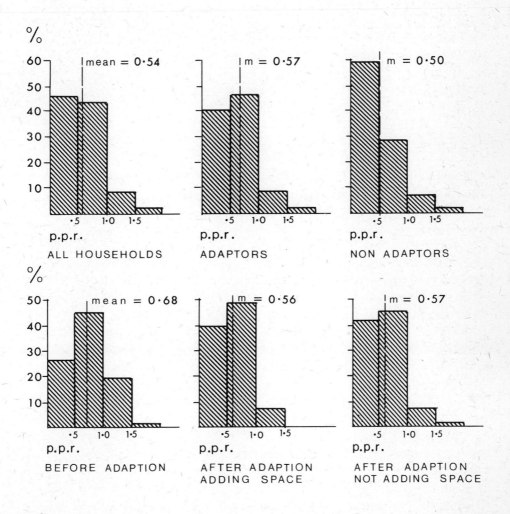

Figure 8.5   Distribution of occupancy rates for adaptors and non-adaptors

Table 8.8

Ppr by type of space added

ppr	Type of space added					Reasons given for adaptions					
						By those adding space			By those not adding space		
	Bedroom	Livingroom	Kitchen Diner	Sunroom	Other	A	B	C	A	B	C
0·0 −0·49	18%	37%	28%	32%	13%	22%	34%	18%	0%	48%	70%
0·50−0·99	51%	44%	42%	47%	58%	50%	52%	50%	93%	41%	20%
1·0 −1·49	31%	20%	29%	20%	29%	26%	13%	32%	7%	10%	10%
1·5+	0%	0%	1%	0%	0%	0%	0%	0%	0%	0%	0%
Sample size	49	41	72	34	31	76	59	22	14	77	10

A Wanted more space
B Wanted to modernise
C Preferred to adapt rather than move

Physical constraints

In response to an open-ended question concerning the reasons for adaption, 20 per cent of the adapting households stated that they adapted to modernise the dwelling. Twice that number of households said that to 'modernise the dwelling' was the most important reason for adapting. Three-quarters of those adaptors who did not add a room or other space, adapted 'to modernise' their dwelling while over half those adaptors who did add a room or other space in their adaption also adapted 'to modernise'.

Few of the households in the sample suffered from severe physical constraint prior to adaption − they lived in what would generally be considered to be good physical conditions. Only 3 per cent of all the households, and only 1 per cent of the adapting group lacked a bath or internal wc. An equally small proportion of the sample shared rooms or amenities with other households prior to adaption. In our sample, the adaptions involving physical amenities such as bathrooms and wc's, seem to be improvement and modernisation of existing amenities, rather than the addition of an amenity where it had not existed before. No extensive conclusions can be drawn about the effect that physical deficiencies have on an adapting decision. Some 13 per cent adapted 'to conform to taste'. It would appear that it is not the lack of, or the sharing of amenities *per se*, that is a constraint for the adapting households as in the case of moving behaviour, but rather the lack of modern styled amenities to satisfy owner-occupying household expectations.

Constraint and the propensity to adapt

The effects of the interaction of the survey variables on the propensity to adapt were examined using a form of multivariate regression analysis. The methodology was the same as that used in the analysis of constraint by moving behaviour as described in Chapter 6. The dependent variable described the probability of adaption and took the value 1 for those households that had adapted and 0 for those that had not. The independent binary variables used in the analysis are listed below.

1 Age of head of household $<$ or $\geqslant$ than 40 years
2 Socio-economic group equal to SEG I or equal to SEG II, III, IV
3 Size of household $>$ 2 persons or $\leqslant$ 2 persons
4 No children or 1 or more child
5 Presence or absence of other adults in the household
6 Length of stay at present address $<$ 3 years
7 Length of stay 3—10 years or $>$ 10 years
8 Persons per room $<$ 0·50 or $\geqslant$ 0·50
9 Income of head of household $>$ £40 per week or $\leqslant$ £40 per week
10 Date of construction before or after 1919
11 Reason for moving to present dwelling — 'wanted a different area'
12 Reason for moving to present dwelling — 'wanted more living space'
13 Number of bedrooms $\leqslant$ 3 or $>$ 3
14 Lack/share one or more facilities or all facilities available
15 Price of house $<$ £9000 or $\geqslant$ £9000

In addition the following redefined variables were used in the non-interactive regressions:
16 Size of household $>$ 5 or $\leqslant$ 5 persons
17 Persons per room $>$ 1·1 or $\leqslant$ 1·1
18 Price of house $>$ £12,000 or $\leqslant$ £12,000

Some 43 interaction variables were defined, as illustrated in Figure 8.6. Four regressions were run, two using the simple non-interaction variables, two the interaction variables. The first run included the price-of-house variable, the second excluded this variable. The third run again included the price variable, the fourth excluded it. This procedure was adopted to identify the effects of including and excluding the price-of-house variable, because although it was felt to be important, the sample was reduced by two-thirds when this variable was included because of non-response to this question. Tables 8.9 and 8.10 present the results of the two regressions run on the simple non-interactive variables. The figures in parentheses are standard errors.

151

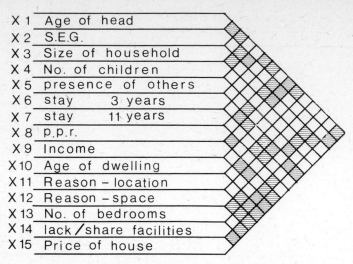

X 1	Age of head
X 2	S.E.G.
X 3	Size of household
X 4	No. of children
X 5	presence of others
X 6	stay 3 years
X 7	stay 11 years
X 8	p.p.r.
X 9	Income
X 10	Age of dwelling
X 11	Reason – location
X 12	Reason – space
X 13	No. of bedrooms
X 14	lack/share facilities
X 15	Price of house

Figure 8.6   Interaction variables

Table 8.9

Results of the non-interaction regression with
price variable included

Independent variables	β–coefficients	
Date of construction before 1919	0·241	
	(0·08)	
Age of head younger than 40 years	−0·222	
	(0·09)	
Reason for move from last home because	0·183	Constant a 0·469
household wanted a different area	(0·108)	Multiple R 0·378
Price of house less than £12,000	0·167	R^2 0·143
	(0·09)	Standard error 0·459
Size of household greater than 5 persons	0·182	F-level $F_{8,112}$ 3·753
	(0·128)	No. of cases 118

Table 8.10

Results of the non-interaction regression without
price variable

Independent variables	β–coefficients	
Size of household 1–2 persons	−0·256	Constant a 0·696
	(0·05)	Multiple R 0·32
Date of construction before 1919	0·111	R^2 0·103
	(0·049)	Standard error 0·461
Length of stay longer than 11 years	−0·136	F-level $F_{3,396}$ 13·25
	(0·058)	No. of cases 350

The following variables appear to affect the probability of adaption:

Positive effects

1 Dwelling built before 1919
2 Households of 5 persons or more
3 Purchase price of house less than £12,000
4 Reason for last move – 'wanted to live in a different area'

Negative effects

1 Head of household less than 40 years old
2 Households of 2 persons or less

It can be seen that cheaper older property, selected because a large household wanted to move to a particular area, and had done so during the last three years, might be a candidate for adaption. On the other hand, if a household was small and had not moved recently, then that property would be less likely to be adapted. The regression analysis using interaction variables produced similar but more sensitive results. The pattern of interaction is illustrated in Tables 8.11 and 8.12. The interaction equations are by their nature more complicated, but by allowing the factors to interact one with another, a higher degree of explanation is achieved. As in the previous section, the inclusion of the price variable again increases the proportion of explained variance, demonstrating the importance of the price of the dwelling, interacting with other factors, in determining whether a household will adapt its dwelling or not.

The interaction regression analysis that includes price, suggests that the following variables positively affect the decision by the household to adapt their dwelling:

1 Date of construction before 1919
2 Date of construction before 1919, interacting with the price of the house below £9000
3 Weekly income of head over £40, interacting with the price of the house below £9000
4 Reason for previous move because the household wanted a different area
5 Reason for previous move because the household wanted more space, interacting with the fact that they lacked or shared a bath or wc after the move.

Three of these factors were also important in the non-interactive regressions: the dwelling being built before 1919, the dwelling being bought

Table 8.11

Results of the interaction regression with price variable included

Independent variables	β—coefficients	
Size of household is 1—2 persons and the age of head less than 40 years	−0·248 (0·89)	
Date of construction before 1919	0·161 (0·10)	
Date of construction before 1919 and the price of the house less than £9000	0·221 (0·14)	
Reason for move from previous house because household wanted a different area	0·232 (0·10)	
Reason for previous move because the household wanted more space, and because they now lack or share a bath or wc	0·526 (0·43)	
Weekly income of head of household over £40 and the price of the house is less than £9000	0·219 (0·13)	Constant a 0·863 Multiple R 0·55
Weekly income of head of household over £40 and SEG is professional or managerial	−0·493 (0·22)	R^2 0·303 Standard error 0·422
Number of bedrooms less than 3	−0·255 (0·11)	F-level 5·216 No. of cases 118

Table 8.12

Results of the interaction regression without price variable

Independent variables	β—coefficients	
Size of household 1—2 persons and number of bedrooms less than 3	−0·100 (0·08)	
Size of household 1—3 persons and lacking/ sharing bath or wc	−0·249 (0·15)	
Presence of other persons over 6 years, and ppr less than 0·5	−0·144 (0·08)	
Date of construction before 1914	0·129 (0·04)	
Length of stay longer than 11 years	−0·130 (0·06)	
Length of stay less than 3 years and age of head less than 40 years	−0·21 (0·08)	Constant a 0·677 Multiple R 0·375
Age of head less than 40 years	0·105 (0·06)	R^2 0·140 Standard error 0·453
Reason for previous move because household wanted a different area	0·205 (0·106)	F-level 6·960 No. of cases 350

154

relatively cheaply and the reason for the previous move (within the last three years) because the household preferred a different area. In addition, the interactive analysis brings to light the fact that if the head of household is earning more than £40 per week, but buys a less expensive property, this will positively affect the future possibility of adaption.

The probability of adaption is negatively affected by the following factors:

1   Size of household is 1–2 persons, interacting with the age of the head of household less than 40 years
2   The weekly income of the head of household is over £40, interacting with an SEG of I or II
3   The number of bedrooms is less than 3

A small household, or a household with a young head of household affects adaption negatively. This can be explained on the grounds that a small household will probably be less constrained within its dwelling, it will probably be more mobile and it is to be expected that households with a young head are less likely to be able to afford to adapt. Factor 2 above indicates a situation where, although the household can afford to adapt, it prefers to choose a more expensive house which it need not adapt. Factor 3 raises the complex issue of how adaption is seen as a response to spatial constraints. The presence of less than three bedrooms affects the probability of adaption negatively. While a major reason for adapting was found to be the need for more space, few adapting households added a bedroom. It can be concluded therefore, that living space, rather than sleeping space, was the more common type of spatial constraint that adaptors responded to in the survey sample.

We may conclude that as expected, the older less expensive, and therefore probably unimproved dwellings, have the greatest likelihood of being adapted. Generally, if the decision to move to the present address was made for non-housing reasons then the greater the likelihood of subsequent adaption. In this respect our results are similar to those of an earlier survey,[1] suggesting that decisions to adapt or improve are commonly made in connection with a decision to move. If a household is at a middle stage in its life cycle, e.g. a household of five or more persons with the head of household over 40 years of age, then these circumstances positively affect the likelihood that they will adapt their dwelling. On the other hand young households show a low propensity to adapt, probably due to their limited financial circumstances. Professional and managerial workers showed a lower propensity to adapt than other social groups, they would appear to prefer to buy more expensive post-war and inter-war homes. Dwellings with three bedrooms or less were not adapted as frequently as larger dwellings. The multivariate analysis of the data has therefore brought to light several important factors that help towards an explanation of adaption behaviour within the survey sample. The following factors affect the probability of adaption:

Positive effects

1   Dwelling built before 1919
2   Purchase price of house less than £9000
3   Factors 1 and 2 occurring together
4   Factor 2, interacting with household head earning more than £40 per week
5   Household of 5 persons or more
6   Reason for last move – 'wanted to live in a different area'
7   Reason for last move – 'wanted more space'
8   Length of stay less than 3 years

Negative effects

1   Households of 2 persons or less
2   Length of stay more than 11 years
3   Head of household less than 40 years old
4   Factors 2 and 3 occurring together
5   Head of household's income over £40 per week and belonging to SEG I or II
6   2 or less bedrooms in dwelling

The types of housing constraint that we have considered in this and the preceding chapters were circumscribed by the scope and form of the available data. Most of this data had been collected by others for quite different purposes to our own. Environmental and locational constraints were particularly unrepresented in the data and constitute an important gap in our investigation. However, the approach and methods used appear to have been successful. The general, if partial picture of the pattern of housing constraint that has emerged, indicates the value of our approach for analysing housing conditions. A number of general housing circumstances would appear to greatly increase the likelihood that housing conditions will be unacceptable to a household, unacceptability being expressed through the propensity to move or the propensity to adapt. These general circumstances are not necessarily constraining in themselves, but their presence does increase the overall probability that housing conditions will be unsatisfactory. Finally, it should be concluded that empirical estimates of the wish and ability to move have a limited long-term usefulness. The types, degrees and combinations of housing constraint that were significant in our analyses are themselves subject to change over time. The access constraints are particularly susceptible to rapid change. Their use in long-term forecasting would be suspect.

Notes

[1] R.M. Kirwan and D.B. Martin, *The Economics of Urban Residential Renewal and Improvement*, Working Paper no. 77, Centre for Environmental Studies, London 1972.

9 The management of obsolescence

In this final chapter, we shall attempt to summarise the ways in which housing obsolescence might be controlled and reduced. The principal aim of this book has been to establish a theoretical framework through which the process of obsolescence may be described and evaluated, and our summary will take the same form. We shall not attempt to produce a list of practical recommendations, nor shall we propose a comprehensive policy for alleviating obsolescence. Instead, we shall give an overview of the vulnerabilities of the housing stock and outline some of the options available to combat housing obsolescence.

Strategies for improvement

Most official studies of housing conditions view dwellings as objects. subject to deterioration and decay.[1] These studies have defined standards of unfitness and have then proceeded to use such standards to estimate the quantity of outdated stock.[2] Studies of this kind rely on visual surveys, usually conducted by health inspectors and building surveyors.[3] Subjective estimates of the useful life of dwellings after improvement are often included. The typical outcome is an inventory of different types of stock in various states of 'unfitness'. These studies do not attempt to evaluate degrees of housing obsolescence directly, but they do assume that age, physical condition and the absence of 'essential' facilities are reliable proxies for housing obsolescence. Such assumptions underlie most current legislation and procedures. While these house condition studies and the assumptions on which they have been based, may be sufficient for immediate practical purposes, they take little account of the underlying social and economic causes of obsolescence. Their explanatory powers are therefore weak.

The physically based view of substandard housing has been reflected in housing improvement policies. Target dates for slum clearance have been advanced and extended again and again. In Britain both major political parties have at one time promised the removal of all obsolete stock, the improvement of all substandard dwellings, and the provision of 'a decent home' for everyone. 'Decent' is, however, a relative term and housing standards are never absolute. Housing expectations have risen: what may have been considered a decent home at the turn of the century is no longer acceptable. We must expect that the development of obsolescence in the future will be as much a consequence of human decision, rising expectations and the operations of the housing market, as of physical deterioration. The nature of obsolescence suggests that the goal of entirely eliminating poor housing is unrealistic. A proportion of the housing stock will be obsolescent whatever policies are adopted, obsolescent that is, relative either to the conditions prevailing in the housing stock as a whole, or to the preferences and expectations of the population. The proportion of relatively poor housing within the stock as a whole, may increase over time, and the gap between good and bad may widen.

Moreover, while we can evaluate current housing circumstances, we cannot predict with any certainty how these circumstances might change beyond a short time horizon; the future rate of housing obsolescence cannot be statistically forecast with any degree of accuracy. We have therefore suggested an approach in which housing obsolescence is viewed as a process of change, a process in which physical unfitness may be the net result, but is not necessarily the cause, of obsolescence. The fundamental nature of the problem argues for a modest approach in which we take incremental actions to prevent further deterioration and to effect gradual improvements over time. The development of obsolescence in housing can be managed, controlled, and reduced, but it will not be eliminated entirely.

The overriding purpose of a housing policy is to work towards a better match between the demands for housing and the supply of dwellings and to achieve a balanced distribution of housing and employment. The management of obsolescence is only concerned with part of this, namely the improvement of the current areas of severe mismatch and the prevention of deteriorating conditions in the future. The strategies for improving housing conditions and reducing obsolescence are therefore of two kinds, corrective and preventative. The first tackles the problems of obsolescence in the current housing stock, with the aim of extending the useful life of existing dwellings and of improving conditions in the worst housing areas. The second acts to reduce the probability of early obsolescence in the new stock that is now being built across the country as a whole, aiming to ensure that today's housing standards do not jeopardise the future unnecessarily. The corrective approach tends therefore, to be basically local and short term in nature, the preventative approach more general and long term.

Corrective measures

Britain has an impressive record of corrective housing legislation. The 1936 Housing Act gave local authorities the power to clear slums, through demolition and closing orders, and enabled them to compel private owners to repair unfit dwellings. In 1949, Improvement Grants for the installation of standard amenities — bath, wc, hot and cold water — were made available if the probable life of a dwelling was estimated to be at least thirty years after improvement. The 1954 Housing Repairs and Rents Act extended slum clearance powers and increased improvement grants, also allowing controlled rents to be raised after improvement. With the exception of the 1957 Rent Act, progressive legislation has continued and was extended in 1964 with the introduction of the notion of Improvement Areas. Following a review of policy concerning slums and older housing, the 1973 White Paper — *Better Homes — The Next Priorities* — shifted the emphasis away from demolition and comprehensive redevelopment towards programmes in which

> ... new building and rehabilitation are carefully integrated, house improvement being used to phase urban renewal in ways which allow continuous, flexible and gradual redevelopment on a relatively small scale.[4]

Within this policy, priorities were redirected towards:

1   Those areas where more houses were in bad condition but where, nevertheless, there was a heavy demand for accommodation, e.g. in central London.
2   Those areas with poor physical and environmental conditions where population was falling and the pressure of demand was low.
3   General improvement areas which were residential districts that were relatively free of stressful conditions, which contained sound older housing which when improved would provide reasonable housing environments for at least thirty years.
4   Essential repairs to individual dwellings, especially those occupied by poorer owners unable to meet the full cost of such work.

In addition, legislation was established for the declaration of Housing Action Areas through which the existing legislation could be extended and applied in a comprehensive manner to deal with the physical conditions in the very worst areas of housing, including recommending changes for short-term use of vacant dwellings.

Corrective measures to counteract housing obsolescence in the short term will take place in the main within this existing legislative framework. The existing array of households in dwellings, together with the structure of housing institutions and markets, offer considerable inertia to change. They can be modified marginally, but fundamental changes are rarely possible in the short term. Our national economic circumstances also make drastic change unlikely. The optimistic forecasts of the recent past have now given way to a very cautious interpretation of the existing housing legislation. Large-scale redevelopment has been discounted in favour of small-scale incremental improvement and the aim of clearing the slums has given way to 'improving' them. In these circumstances in which a significant increase in national housing expenditure is unlikely, and given the existing housing institutions, three principal options are possible to correct the development of obsolescence in the short term:

1   Measures that aim to reduce households' dissatisfaction with their housing conditions, by
   (a)   acting to modify the 'effects' of existing levels of housing constraint by influencing households' expectations,
   (b)   acting to remove the worst housing conditions at the expense of those households who are in generally 'unsatisfactory' but not 'intolerable' conditions,
   (c)   acting differentially to reduce those types of individual constraint that give rise to the greatest degrees of dissatisfaction at the expense of those constraints which do not appear to be so critical.
2   Measures that enable and stimulate individual households to respond to poor housing circumstances, by
   (a)   acting to assist households to move to dwellings and locations which entail lower levels of housing constraint,
   (b)   acting to help households to modify and improve the standards of their accommodation.
3   Measures that improve the mechanisms and procedures through which households are allocated to dwellings so that more efficient use is made of the existing stock.

With the current economic circumstances, option 1a above could be adopted to influence household perceptions of what constitutes unsatisfactory conditions and to make households aware that some degree of dissatisfaction is unavoidable at this time. In this way the growth in housing expectations might be retarded, particularly for those who are already fortunate enough to live in tolerable if not desirable conditions. This is an unattractive argument for reducing housing expectations in the short term but, in times of economic difficulty, it is already a common approach in respect to income and consumption generally. It is likely however, that housing consumption could only be postponed for a short time, and option 1a might increase the problems of obsolescence in the long term. This measure could perhaps be justified if all of the financial resources available for housing improvement were to be redirected strictly towards the very worst areas of intolerable housing constraint, option 1b above.

With this strategy, general Improvement Area designations would cease temporarily and professional efforts would be applied to Housing Action Area designation and improvement. The Action Area legislation envisaged that a series of criteria would be developed, on the basis of which areas for housing action and improvement would be identified. It was anticipated that the incidence of overcrowding, furnished tenancies, shared accommodation, elderly people, large families and housing lacking basic facilities might indicate areas of housing stress.[4] Our analysis of housing constraint confirmed that all of these factors, together with others, are important indicators of very poor conditions and obsolescence. In the univariate and multivariate analyses of both moving and adapting behaviour, accommodation in pre-1919 dwellings significantly increased the likelihood that households would find the accommodation to be unsatisfactory. This was the most major and irreversible factor underlying poor housing conditions. The distribution of areas with a high proportion of pre-1919 dwellings in the Greater London area is shown in figure 9.1 In levels 4 and 5, the darker areas, over 58 and 78 per cent respectively, of the housing stock in a ward was built before 1919. The results of our analyses suggest that those wards within these areas that also contain high proportions of privately rented accommodation that is both shared and overcrowded, are those that give rise to the most intolerable conditions. It is the combination of constraints in these areas to which option 1b would relate.

While it may be expedient to deal with the very worst problems first, it is an assumption of our approach that adequate housing standards for all will continue to be an important long-term goal. Without an increase in the level of housing resources, only one further option is theoretically available, to shift the balance in constraint relaxation towards those individual types of constraint which can be shown to be the most important contributors to dissatisfaction. With this option, 1c above, we need to examine the relative importance of each constraint in turn and distinguish those that are more critical. The results of our investigation suggest that the spatial constraint resulting from the size of dwelling and the size of household as expressed through the ratio of persons per room is the most critical single constraint acting. The probability of dissatisfaction with

162

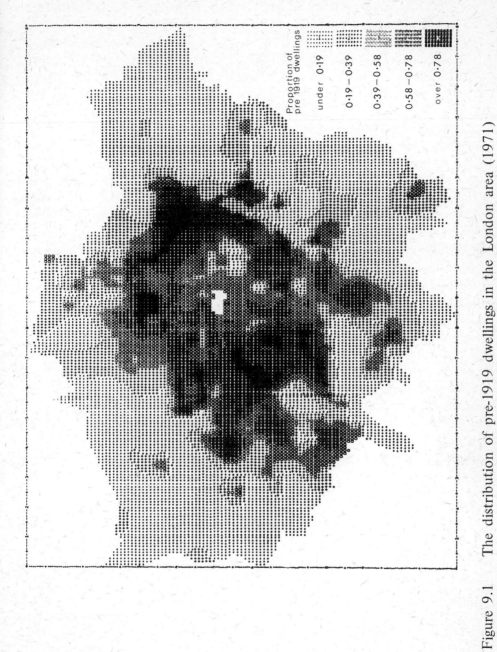

Proportion of
pre 1919 dwellings

under 0·19

0·19 — 0·39

0·39 — 0·58

0·58 — 0·78

over 0·78

Figure 9.1   The distribution of pre-1919 dwellings in the London area (1971)

163

housing conditions increased rapidly with occupancy rates of about 1·0 ppr. Spatial constraint also appears to be an important determinant of adapting behaviour. The other housing circumstances affecting the likelihood of serious dissatisfaction concern the shared use of dwellings and the lack or shared use of basic facilities.

An analysis of the 1966 and 1971 Census data showed that the absence-of-bath variable was very highly correlated ($r = 0·97$) with the other facility variables, indicating that the absence of a bath is of prime importance in identifying deficient facilities generally. Figures 9.2 and 9.3 show the distribution of dwellings lacking baths and the distribution of households sharing accommodation. In Figure 9.2, level 5, the darkest area identifies the wards in the GLC area in which more than 24 per cent of dwellings are without a fixed bath. In Figure 9.3, the darkest area indicates those wards in which more than 32 per cent of households are sharing accommodation. It is interesting to note the different spatial distribution of these two constraints in the London area. While no specific surveys have been completed to discriminate between the effects of all the different types of housing constraint in a comprehensive way, we would suggest that with the available evidence, priority should be given to the reduction of the constraints associated with overcrowding, sharing and dwellings lacking basic facilities.

We shall next consider the corrective measures that may be available under option 2, to encourage individual households to reduce their housing constraints through moving or adapting. Most households undertake adaptions or move without the help of any outside agency, be it the State or a local housing action group. However, many households who could benefit from moving or adaption are either financially unable to do so, or do not realise the improved housing conditions that could be achieved by so doing. We have seen that moving is the most common way in which households improve their residential conditions. There are three ways in which the propensity to move can be influenced:

1   Measures can be taken to help households recognise the existing possibilities of improvement through moving.
2   Measures can be taken to increase the financial ability to move for those households in poor housing conditions.
3   New types of dwelling and tenure could be developed to overcome the supply constraints due to the lack of suitable alternative accommodation and limited choice in the existing stock.

Information about the advantages and disadvantages of moving, in response to poor housing conditions, is scarce. While there has been a

164

Proportion
without bath

under 0·06

0·06 — 0·12

0·12 — 0·18

0·18 — 0·24

over 0·24

Figure 9.2   The distribution of dwellings without a bath in the London area (1971)

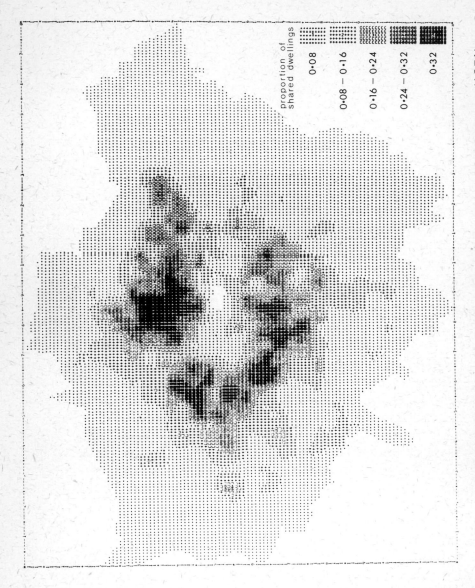

proportion of
shared dwellings

0·08

0·08 – 0·16

0·16 – 0·24

0·24 – 0·32

0·32

Figure 9.3   The distribution of households sharing accommodation in the London area (1971)

166

dramatic increase in the number of local housing action groups and advice centres, these organisations have not generally provided information concerning work and housing opportunities in other areas. These groups can act against the interest of poorer households if they assume that the social structure of an area should be preserved at all costs, and do not therefore help households to consider the more drastic action of moving away from an area altogether. There is an urgent need for co-ordinated housing and employment bureaus in our major cities, to supplement the work of housing advice centres with information about the opportunities available in other locations.

The majority of households in areas of poor housing are financially unable to move to better accommodation. They are unable to meet the relevant access criteria, as described in Chapter 7, and so move to better-quality stock and different forms of tenure; often alternative dwellings are simply not available. With the rapid cost of building materials and labour, the gap between 'housing costs' and the 'ability to pay' has widened considerably. This is particularly so in the owner-occupied sector. Since it is unlikely that the costs of materials and labour will drop relative to household income, measures to relax access constraints in this sector will involve changes to the current system of finance. Two important allowances are given to owner-occupiers when they purchase a dwelling with mortgage finance. A proportion of mortgage interest payments may be set against tax liabilities, and no tax is levied on any capital gain received on the subsequent sale. If the access criteria to the owner-occupied sector are to be eased then some redistribution of these allowances will be necessary to first-time buyers. This is a problem of taxation policy, which would require detailed analysis. However, it is probable that changes in the tax allowances would only assist those households who are currently on the margin of owner-occupation; it is unlikely that low-income groups could, with present costs, be assisted to enter the sector *en masse*.

Since the owner-occupied sector is closed to many households, and the private rented sector is diminishing, it is access to the local authority sector that is currently under most pressure. Here allocation is managed. Access is limited by the amount of accommodation available rather than the ability to pay. The current excess of demand over supply could be reduced in one of three ways: first, by a massive extension of the public rented sector through new building and the compulsory purchase of private rented accommodation; secondly, by reforming the financial framework of the public sector to redistribute subsidies to low-income families while at the same time taking measures to resuscitate the private rented sector; thirdly, through alternative forms of tenure that would increase the range of choice in housing. Given that there is an existing imbalance between the costs of the provision and maintenance of public housing and rent income, the first alternative is unlikely to be possible in the short term. The second alternative, involving the redistribution of subsidies, is a political issue which may be important to, but is not part of, the specific problem of managing housing obsolescence. The third possibility, that of introducing alternative forms of tenure, is theoretically most attractive.

The object of innovations of this kind is to reduce inequalities between households living in different forms of housing tenure, both for the sake of greater fairness and to give more choice and variety to households at each stage of their life cycle. A start has already been made in the diversification of tenure. A 1973 White Paper laid down the basis for the expansion of the voluntary housing movement and encouraged the formation of housing associations to prove a further alternative in the rented sector.[5] The White Paper also encouraged the provision of accommodation for small households and those with special needs, e.g. single-person households, the elderly and the handicapped. More recently, with the increase in homelessness in our major cities, 'ready access' stock and 'short term' tenure have been proposed as alternatives to private rented accommodation.[6] More fundamentally, it is important to note that in Britain households have either 100 per cent equity stake in their dwelling (owner-occupiers) or a nil equity stake (the rented sector). It is not difficult to imagine future systems of tenure in which households would have a choice to take an equity stake from 0–100 per cent in their dwelling, so merging the renting and owning concepts. Furthermore, it would be possible to arrange for the percentage equity stake to change with time, e.g. retiring households might wish to change from a 100 per cent to a 0 per cent stake, receiving the capital sum and paying rent for the remainder of their life. On the other hand, young households might wish to increase their percentage equity stake as their income and family circumstances change.

The second type of action that owners and landlords may be encouraged to take is that of improving substandard dwellings. In the owner-occupied sector, improvement activity is at a high level. In our survey of improvements and conversions, more than 40 per cent of the random control sample had undertaken adaptions of one kind or another. A surprising proportion of those households who had improved their dwellings had undertaken some of the adaption work themselves in order to reduce expenditure (see Table 8.7). More households could be encouraged to do this if local authorities provided housing improvement and advice services, perhaps under the guidance of the National Building Agency. In this way,

168

for a nominal cost, lower-income households could gain access to professional advice, and the standards and types of the improvements undertaken could be better controlled. However, the major task should be to encourage improvement activity in more obsolescent stock.

The improvement grant system lies at the centre of current policy concerning the modernisation and adaption of deficient stock. It has become increasingly clear that this system, while an important innovation in principle, has tended to act regressively. Our survey, and those of others,[7] has showed that in owner-occupied housing, households who had received improvement grants were not those, in the main, with low income or those in the worst housing conditions, neither were their dwellings amongst the most obsolescent stock. This is perhaps not surprising. Any improvement grant criteria which refer solely to general types of improvement are unlikely to channel funds to poorer households since the dwellings that are eligible for the grant become attractive to the middle-income groups who are able to improve their housing conditions subsidised by the State. Moreover, the provision of improvement grants to landlords in areas of poor housing has not tended to benefit the occupants of the area. It has lead to the displacement of low-income households due to the sale of private rented property for owner occupation.

If the improvement grant system is to become more effective in reducing obsolescence and if the undesirable side effects of the present system are to be avoided, then the criteria for allocating funds must be of a more discriminating kind. Firstly, funds should be directed towards the most obsolescent stock that is capable of improvement; improvement grants should not necessarily be available in all housing areas. Secondly, funds should only be directed to the more essential improvements such as structural stability, weatherproofing and major repairs. Thirdly, funds could be directed towards those households least able to afford to pay for improvements themselves. Improvement grants could be made progressive, with larger grants of up to 100 per cent being available to lower-income families in poor accommodation, while higher-income households in dwellings needing improvement would receive a much reduced percentage. While these measures would involve some form of means test it would help to channel funds to the worst housing circumstances where improvement is least likely. Finally, it might be possible to encourage tenants to improve their dwellings in the worst housing areas by enabling them to take the initiative for improvement, backed up by an improvement loan or grant system. A system of this kind, in which the tenant as well as the landlord takes the initiative for improvement, would have the benefit of enabling tenants to influence the sort of improvement undertaken. This would result in the constraints as perceived by the tenants being more effectively alleviated than at present.

Many of the short-term corrective measures that could reduce the current levels of housing obsolescence have now been briefly mentioned. One major option remains. The allocation of households to dwellings, in both the private and public sectors, could be modified or restructured in order that better use is made of the existing housing stock and so that aggregate conditions are improved. In many areas the demand for housing exceeds the supply. This leads to rising rents, multi-occupation and over-crowding in the private rented sector, to acute scarcity and unrealistically long waiting lists in the public housing sector, and to high property values that exclude younger households from owner-occupation. It is not impossible for the extremes of imbalance to occur simultaneously in one locality, with high overcrowding in stock under one form of tenancy while stock under a different tenancy is subject to high vacancy rates. The rapid contraction of the private rented sector following the recently introduced controls over rent and security of tenure has led to homelessness, squatting and a severe shortage of accommodation for single-person households, single-parent families and households who do not meet local authority residence qualifications. It is these imbalances between the distribution of housing and households that underlie many local housing problems.

Recently there has been an increasing mismatch between the size of households and size of dwellings. The 1971 Census shows a higher proportion of large households in small dwellings in central urban areas and relative underoccupation in suburban and rural areas. Figure 9.4 shows the distribution of overcrowding in the GLC area based on the Census definition of 1·5 ppr. Figure 9.5 shows the distribution of those households living at greater than 1·0 ppr, the level at which most households become seriously dissatisfied with their housing conditions for spatial reasons. A comparison of Figures 9.4 and 9.5 shows the degree to which the official standard of overcrowding underestimates the severity of this factor. Figure 9.6 shows the distribution of households living at less than 0·5 ppr. The darkest area, level 5, indicates those wards in which more than 36 per cent of the housing stock is underoccupied to this extent. London, quite clearly, has a considerable quantitative surplus of housing space but its distribution does not correspond to the pattern of demand.

There is a vacuum in policy concerning the mismatch between the size of households and dwellings. In the owner-occupied sector there are no incentives for small retired households to move to smaller accommodation and so release their larger dwellings onto the market: in fact there is often no such alternative accommodation available. In the local authority sector

170

Figure 9.4   Households living at more than 1·5 ppr in the London area (1971)

171

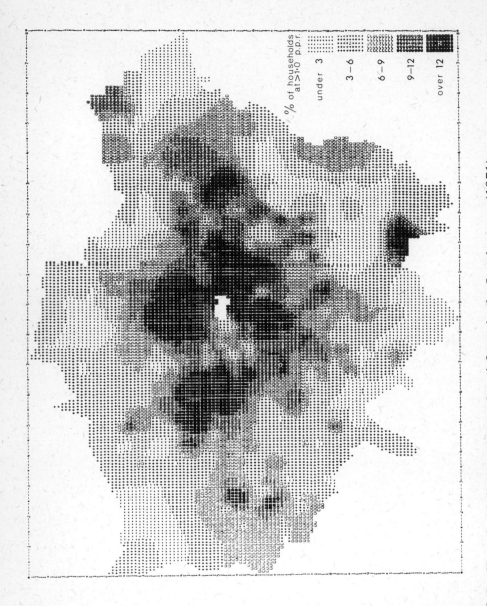

% of households
at ≥1·0 p.p.r.

under 3
3 – 6
6 – 9
9–12
over 12

Figure 9.5   Households living at more than 1·0 ppr in the London area (1971)

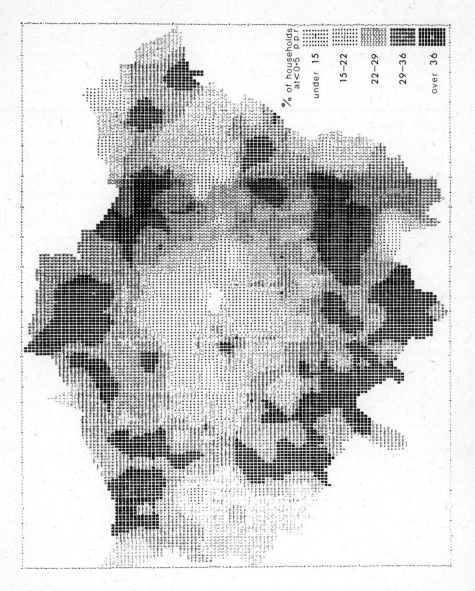

Figure 9.6   Households living at less than 0·5 ppr in the London area (1971)

173

some councils have decided to make short-term allocations of vacant stock, especially that awaiting redevelopment, in an effort to reduce homelessness, but there is no co-ordinated policy. While the social benefit of using vacant stock is clear, the social costs of squatting by those who could afford to rent available accommodation are considerable; squatting by those that are not homeless, in the real sense of the word, has retarded the housing programmes of some inner London boroughs. Government policy has assumed that all housing problems are local problems and there is therefore no need for national and regional housing location policy. This may be a politically convenient stance for central government to take but it is difficult to see how the excessive demands for housing in some areas and the excessive vacancy rate in others can be brought into better balance through local action alone. We would anticipate, given the continuation of the slight national housing surplus, that the imbalances between the distribution of housing and households, at both regional and local levels, will be seen as the outstanding cause of unsatisfactory conditions during the rest of this century.

Without some policy framework with which to reduce this basic imbalance, it is probable that none of the corrective measures that have been described could lead to significant reductions in housing obsolescence if they were to be adopted singly. A variety of measures need to be incorporated within an integrated improvement strategy, depending on the local housing circumstances. The politicians have already produced a framework within which some short-term corrective measures may be taken to reduce obsolescence. If this corrective legislation is to be fully implemented we need to agree on a comprehensive system for monitoring housing conditions, we need to develop methods for converging on, and identifying, those housing areas that contain the most obsolescent stock and give rise to high levels of housing stress.

One major theoretical shortcoming that inhibits progress in this respect is the lack of a system of housing indicators. Many different types of social indicators have been developed; evaluative and predictive indicators, operations and programme indicators, monitoring and output indicators, indicators of demand and supply. While individual indicators are rarely reliable in a statistical sense it is expected that composite indices will eventually provide a powerful way of detecting situations where prompt remedial action is required.[8] In housing, no collection of suitable indicators have yet been combined to form a reliable means for assessing conditions in order to discriminate between different degrees of housing stress. The GLC Index of Housing Stress was an early example of this kind of approach.[9] This index is based on seven variables, weighted according

174

to their supposed importance. Both the variables and the weightings were selected subjectively by the GLC Planning Department. The seven variables were derived from three basic Census variables, describing overcrowding, sharing and lack of physical facilities. Several of the variables comprising the index are highly correlated with each other, and the simple arithmetic used in compiling the index gives rise to a degree of double counting. As a result, doubts have been expressed and an alternative method of weighting the variables through imputed rent has been examined, but this also has some acknowledged deficiencies.[10]

At present in Britain there is no methodology whereby local planning and housing departments can monitor the impact of their policies and decisions. The basic components of a model to simulate and monitor obsolescence were described in Chapter 5 (see Figure 5.4), and some quantitative indicators of improvement and deterioration were listed. This description covers only a small part of the housing problem however. We must be careful to distinguish between the problems caused by low income and poverty and those of housing obsolescence *per se*, the former underlying most housing problems. For example, our correlation and factor analyses of the 1966 and 1971 Census data found that the worst housing conditions had a high positive correlation with the unemployed-males and immigrant variables, with coefficients in the range of 0·72 to 0·83. A wide range of indicators will therefore be required to monitor housing conditions.

A considerable amount of statistical information is available concerning the current circumstances of the housing sector at national, regional and district levels. These are aggregated, and general statistics compiled by the government from information provided periodically by the construction industry, the housing authorities and the national Census. Only the Census data can be used for small-area analysis; however, from time to time the various local authorities undertake 'one-off' detailed investigations of housing conditions and opportunities in their area prior to action within the current housing legislation. It is clearly unrealistic to assume that these authorities will be able to conduct comprehensive surveys of housing conditions in all areas prior to action. A major purpose of social indicators would be to bridge the gap between general statistical information on housing conditions and the identification and selection of particular problem areas that warrant detailed local investigation. We suggest therefore, that in developing composite indicators, whether of housing stress or obsolescence, greater weight should be given to the practical criteria of decision taking rather than to the more academic requirements associated with the development of social statistics.

There would be two basic reference points in our approach: an inventory and description of the general statistical information available, and a detailed account of the aims, objectives and criteria of the various actions that are possible under current housing legislation. The 'bridge building' between these two reference points is unlikely to be achieved by a single all-purpose index comprising a number of weighted variables as in the case of the GLC Stress Index. We would suggest that an alternative methodology should be employed based on a multistage approach in which the housing areas under consideration would be progressively subdivided through the discriminatory powers of individual constraints or small groups of constraints, dependent on the particular aims of exercise. In this way it should be possible to converge on the areas where individual local investigations are warranted under the various sections of the Housing Acts.

Preventative measures

The main emphasis of recent housing policy has been directed to corrective rather than preventative measures. When existing dwellings are demolished and replaced, then expensive housing is substituted for cheaper dwellings. It is therefore sensible to conserve the existing stock wherever possible, through improvement rather than redevelopment. However, a corrective policy of incremental improvement should not be allowed to jeopardise long-term conditions. Some demolition and redevelopment is necessary and the possible repercussions that newer housing might hold for the incidence and rate of future obsolescence should be considered.

Much of the improvement that has been achieved in areas of substandard housing has only been possible because of the character of the stock inherited from the last century. In the main, this occupies central and therefore relatively desirable locations. Its size and form has facilitated conversion and adaption. Its standard of construction, involving considerable structural redundancy, has eased the problems of maintenance and has increased the possibilities for improvement. The history of this type of stock illustrates its inherent potential for change. During its life much of this stock has served households with widely different incomes, it has supported different forms of tenure, and it has often permitted changes away from residential use to support office, educational and retail functions. The newer housing stock will not offer similar opportunities for change and improvement in the twenty-first century. In order to prevent early obsolescence we should try to assess the long-term vulnerability of the new stock and reduce the risk of social, economic, physical and locational failures of one kind or another.

While the standards of our worst housing have steadily improved as a result of the corrective measures that have been undertaken, the housing standards in the stock as a whole are probably on the decline, and are certainly not rising. Over half of the existing housing stock has been built during the last thirty years. Throughout this period, design standards have limited the range of housing produced and constructional standards have tended to drop as a result of cost cutting and the short-term expediency of the housing programme. This is most apparent in the standard of materials used. The onset of physical decay and obsolescence can be controlled almost indefinitely, given adequate maintenance and provided that the major building elements are sound. The reduction in the standards of traditional forms of construction and the introduction of industrialised building systems have both increased the risk of earlier obsolescence. For example, it is probable that the combination of poor-quality material and the much reduced structural timber sizes of modern domestic roof construction will necessitate complete roof replacement long before the average life span of our current stock. This will not be the type of maintenance problem with which owners and landlords are familiar, involving relatively small amounts of incremental expenditure year by year. The magnitude of the costs involved will, in most cases, compel borrowing. Many households and landlords may postpone such expenditure, particularly since dwellings will be uninhabitable while such improvements are being made. The effects will be particularly acute in estates of similar houses where they may lead to rapid decay and obsolescence.

This is only one example, but other modern standards carry similar risk and there are many reasons for a pessimistic view. The imposition of one set of minimum standards, following the Parker Morris Report[11] and the publication of *Space in the Home*,[12] has led to uniformity in the housing produced during the last decade. The evidence given to the Parker Morris Committee was clear, '. . . additional floor space takes first priority in the evidence' and 'the adaptable house . . . is a recurring theme in the evidence we received'. However, the standards that resulted from this investigation gave only a marginal increase of approximately 12 square feet per person in gross floor area, with no requirement for in-built flexibility. 'Space in the home' implies a ppr ratio of not less than 1·0, and the room sizes that are illustrated — both in living areas and in bedrooms in particular — are smaller than those of most older dwellings. Our analyses concerning the reasons for moving and adapting, and the results of published social surveys, all indicate that the amount of space is the most common cause of dissatisfaction in housing, even for those whose conditions are well within current minimum standards. While the standards of the services and equipment in modern homes have improved considerably, this has been at the expense of basic living space. Services and equipment such as central heating, fitted kitchens, rewiring, etc. are easily added to dwellings, but additional space is more difficult and expensive to provide later. If housing expectations and standards continue to rise it is difficult to see how most of our newer homes will be able to expand and adapt.

Others have come to the same conclusion, that dwelling size and the lack of adaptability will '. . . condemn even recently built properties to an earlier obsolescence than one would normally expect'.[13] The basic Parker Morris house, with its priorities towards fitted equipment and services and away from ample space, does not provide a suitable stage-set for improvements which will be necessary in the future.

Modern standards have also led to a reduction in the range of accommodation available, and has created the 'typical' modern house — 'five rooms, three up and two down' — built in estates to minimum internal space standards and with very small gardens. This new stock is increasingly out of step with changes in household structure and size. 'The standard form of a three bedroom house, dictated partly by policy in the public sector and, in the private, partly by the demand of families at particular stages of the family cycle who constitute the main bulk of the house-buyers, has resulted in a housing stock of increasing rigidity, out of keeping with contemporary trends in household sizes'.[14] Unlike older stock, the modern house cannot be readily converted into smaller self-contained units.

The new housing stock is also being designed and built within a rigid tenure framework. Architects seem quite happy to work within the local authority housing/private housing schema, assuming that when built the stock will remain within its tenure class throughout its life. The financial and administrative aspects of housing tenure are highly susceptible to change and yet the particular tenure patterns of today are being ossified in the new housing stock. Designers further fragment their view of housing into 'luxury' and 'economy' categories in the private sector. If new stock in an area is closely tailored to one income group and one class of tenure, then it will not be responsive to the changing circumstances of demand.

The location of the newer housing stock may also have important consequences for obsolescence. Most new housing to buy, except that in new towns, has been located in a pragmatic way that reflects the pressures of land scarcity rather than any coherent location policy. Much of this new stock is therefore particularly vulnerable to locational obsolescence. Many private dwellings built in the last ten years are car dependent in that they are not viable housing units for households without a car. The costs of running a car are, in these circumstances, a necessary and growing element of housing expenditure. Should private and public transport costs continue to escalate then it is not difficult to imagine whole areas of newer 'commuter' housing becoming increasingly less attractive with time, due to the higher economic constraints they impose. Successive governments have allowed locational housing problems to go unchecked. We need to understand and explain the attributes that contribute to locational disutility and obsolescence so that the set of unsuitable or 'risk' locations can be identified together with the residue that appear to be reasonably satisfactory. We need to develop effective tools for evaluating areas of locational housing stress in order to investigate the long-term locational repercussions of alternative housing strategies in new planning proposals.

While our analysis of housing constraint and moving behaviour could not pick up the effects of the more recent housing, we found that the probability of a household wanting to move for housing reasons was higher for those in post-war dwellings than for those occupying inter-war stock, both in the London and Birmingham areas. There appears to be little evidence that households actively prefer post-war homes to older ones. The standards of our new housing are deficient in many important respects, they do not appear to meet even the requirements of households today. From the standpoint of size, variety, construction, tenure and location the newer stock seems likely to restrict the range of options and responses to obsolescence as it develops in the future. Housing standards should be fundamentally reconsidered, diversified and redirected towards those aspects that will be difficult to reverse and correct.

The future degree of balance or imbalance between households and dwellings will depend principally on three factors:

1 Absolute changes in demographic structure and relative changes in households' demands, preferences and expectations.
2 Absolute changes made to the types, quantities and qualities of dwellings in the national stock.
3 Changes in the ways in which households are allocated to dwellings.

Factor 1 is largely uncontrollable. Changes in households' demands cannot be forecast with any reliability and a normative planning approach which attempts to survey present requirements and predict future demands as a basis for decisions concerning the supply of new dwellings is therefore unlikely to help prevent obsolescence. Such an approach may even exaggerate obsolescence by too closely tailoring the new stock to present-day standards and expectations. In contrast, factor 2 is controllable; it involves a long-term concern for the future quality of housing stock and is the responsibility of the relevant professions and the State. Factor 3, the allocation problem, is basically political in nature. It is concerned with the removal of inequity, redistribution of housing resources, the efficient use of the existing stock and the short-term improvement of housing conditions generally. In these circumstances, and if our diagnosis of present shortcomings is reasonably correct, then the most pressing task is to undertake a comprehensive review of the ways in which our current standards, policies and procedures affect factors 2 and 3 above in such a way that future changes within factor 1 are jeopardised. A different approach to 'standard setting' and the control of new development will be needed if these guidelines are to be truly dynamic. The revised standards should be contingent over a wide range of possible changes in future demand. They must ensure as far as possible that the new stock is flexible and adaptable in the widest sense.

The notion that obsolescence may be reduced by built-in flexibility is very old indeed. The adaptability potential of a dwelling or area of housing is closely related to the probability of it becoming obsolete. Some dwelling types may only be utilised in a very limited number of ways while others are capable of adaption to meet a wide range of household circumstances and preferences. The basic structural and spatial form of the dwelling sets the boundary between possible and impossible uses. Different dwellings offer different opportunities for change and modification depending on the materials, constructional methods and building systems used. Physical adaptability is but a small part of the problem however. The demographic characteristics of an area will change during the life of the stock as will the ability of households to rent or buy. New housing should be able to respond and be flexible to different systems of tenure and finance. Changes out of and into residential use should also be possible. Finally, this latent potential for change must be made explicit to future occupants and administrators.

This is not a novel view. Contingency design principles have already received some attention. The notion of indeterminacy has been used to face the unpredictable changes and growth to which organisations and buildings are subject.[15] The theoretical basis for making robust decisions in indeterminate circumstances is well advanced.[16] The development of 'failure planning', negative planning to avoid failures in our policies, buildings and cities, has begun.[17] There are practical examples at the architectural and planning levels,[18],[19] and recent professional concern has jelled within the notion of 'Long life/Loose fit/Low energy' buildings.[20] The beginnings of a new attitude are therefore being established which, if applied to housing, could improve the effectiveness of the new stock to adapt physically, spatially, tenurally and financially as circumstances change. Through further research, development and practical experimentation, we would hope that the utility of the new housing stock could be drastically increased and the risk of obsolescence reduced.

Notes

[1] T.L.C. Duncan, *Measuring Housing Quality*, Occasional paper no. 20, Centre for Urban and Regional Studies, University of Birmingham, 1971.

[2] W.S. Grigson, 'The obsolescence and ageing of London's housing', *GLC Intelligence Unit Quarterly Bulletin*, no. 24, September 1973.

[3] Ministry of Housing and Local Government, *House Condition Surveys,* London, HMSO, 1970.

[4] *Better Homes — The Next Priorities*, Cmnd. 5339, June 1973.

[5] *Widening The Choice: The Next Steps in Housing*, Cmnd. 5280, April 1973.

[6] G. Dimson, 'Best laid schemes. . .', *Built Environment*, vol. 1, no. 1, June 1975.

[7] R.M. Kirwan and D.B. Martin, *The Economics of Urban Residential Renewal and Improvement*, Working paper, no. 77, Centre for Environmental Studies, London 1972.

[8] General Statistical Office, *Social Trends*, no. 1, 1970.

[9] GLC Planning Department, 'Analysis of areas of housing stress', Letter and explanatory appendix to local authorities concerning the analysis of Census data, February 1968.

[10] B.J. Parker, 'The Identification of Areas of Housing' in *Housing Models*, Planning and Transport Research and Computation Ltd, London February 1970.

[11] Parker Morris Report, *Homes for Today and Tomorrow*, Subcommittee of the Central Housing Advisory Committee, HMSO, London 1961.

[12] Ministry of Housing and Local Government, *Space in the Home*, HMSO, London 1963.

[13] C. Buchanan, and Partners, 'The prospect for housing: A Study for the Nationwide Building Society', Nationwide Building Society, London 1971.

[14] W.V. Hole and M.T. Pountney, *Trends in Population, Housing and Occupancy Rates, 1861–1961*, HMSO, London 1971.

[15] J. Weeks, 'Indeterminate architecture', *Transactions of the Bartlett Society*, vol. 2, 1963–4.

[16] J. Rosenhead, M. Elton, S. Gupta, 'Robustness and Optimality as Criteria for Strategic Decisions', *Operations Research Quarterly*, vol. 23, 1972, pp. 413–31.

[17] B.B. Nutt, 'Failure planning', *Architectural Design*, vol. 40, September 1970, pp. 469–71.

[18] J. Weeks, 'Hospitals for the 1970's', *Hospital and Health Management*, RIBA Journal, vol. 71, December 1964.

[19] Milton Keynes Development Corporation, 'The Plan for Milton Keynes', vols. I and II, Warendon, March 1970.

[20] 'The "Long Life, Loose Fit, Low Energy" Study' launched in May 1972 by Alex Gordon when president of the Royal Institute of British Architects.

Appendix A Simulation programmes

J.U.P.R. HOUSING OBSOLESCENCE STUDY : SIMULATION OF
HOUSEHOLD ALLOCATION – VERSION A

SUBROUTINES REQUIRED WITH THE MAIN PROGRAMME
    LA01A
    MCO3AS – THIS SUBROUTINE IS WRITTEN IN ASSEMBLER LANGUAGE
    PROUT

VARIABLES READ FROM THE PROBLEM CARD:
    NH – NUMBER OF HOUSEHOLD CLASSES
    ND – NUMBER OF DWELLING CLASSES
  ITER – NUMBER OF ITERATIONS FOR WHICH THE PROGRAMME IS
        TO BE RUN
   IN1 – INDICATOR 1; IN1=0 THE NUMBER OF HOUSEHOLDS AND
                        STOCK IN EACH CLASS WILL REMAIN
                        CONSTANT
                  IN1=1 THE NUMBER OF HOUSEHOLDS IN EACH
                        CLASS AND THE NUMBER OF DWELLINGS
                        IN EACH CLASS WILL BE CHANGED BY A
                        CONSTANT PROPORTION AT EACH
                        ITERATION
                  IN1=2 THE NUMBER OF HOUSEHOLDS AND
                        DWELLINGS IN EACH CLASS WILL BE
                        CHANGED BY AN AMOUNT WHICH IS
                        READ IN AT EACH ITERATION
   IN2 – INDICATOR 2; IN2=0 PURCHASING ABILITIES REMAIN
                        CONSTANT
                  IN2=1 NEW PURCHASING ABILITIES ARE READ
                        IN AT EACH ITERATION

DATA:
     H – A 1-DIMENSIONAL ARRAY OF LENGTH NH* (ND+1) CONTAINING
        THE NUMBER OF HOUSEHOLDS IN EACH HOUSING SITUATION

A — A 1-DIMENSIONAL ARRAY OF LENGTH NH* (ND+1) CONTAINING THE PROPORTION OF HOUSEHOLDS IN EACH HOUSING SITUATION WHO WOULD LIKE TO MOVE

R — A 1-DIMENSIONAL ARRAY OF LENGTH NH*ND CONTAINING THE OCCUPANCY RATE FOR EACH HOUSING SITUATION

V — A 1-DIMENSIONAL ARRAY OF LENGTH ND CONTAINING THE NUMBER OF INITIALLY VACANT DWELLINGS OF EACH TYPE

E — ARRAY OF LENGTH NH* (ND+1) — ANNUAL COST OF DWELLINGS

Y — ARRAY OF LENGTH NH — MAXIMUM ANN. HOUSING EXP.

DH,DD — ARRAYS OF LENGTH NH AND ND RESPECTIVELY DEFINING CHANGES TO HOUSEHOLDS AND STOCK

B — A 1-DIMENSIONAL ARRAY OF LENGTH NH*ND DEFINING PURCHASING ABILITIES

NOTE: NH* (ND+1) MUST NOT BE GREATER THAN 100

PARAMETERS OF SUBROUTINE LAO1A:

NS — NUMBER OF VARIABLES   NS=NH* (ND+1)

NI — NUMBER OF INEQUALITY CONSTRAINTS   NI=NS+ND+1

NC — TOTAL NUMBER OF CONSTRAINTS   NC=NH+NI

C — A 2-DIMENSIONAL CONSTRAINT MATRIX

W — A 1-DIMENSIONAL ARRAY CONTAINING THE R.H.S. OF CONSTRAINTS

A — A 1-DIMENSIONAL ARRAY CONTAINING COEFFICIENTS OF THE OBJECTIVE FUNCTION

XN — A 1-DIMENSIONAL ARRAY CONTAINING THE SOLUTION ON RETURN

F — OBJECTIVE ON RETURN

IA — FIRST DIMENSION OF C

J.U.P.R. HOUSING OBSOLESCENCE STUDY : SIMULATION OF
HOUSEHOLD ALLOCATION – VERSION B

SUBROUTINES REQUIRED WITH THE MAIN PROGRAMME:
    MONITR
    PRINT

THE FOLLOWING DATA IS REQUIRED BY THE MAIN PROGRAMME:
    ITER – THE NUMBER OF ITERATIONS FOR WHICH THE SIMULATION
            IS TO RUN
    NH   – THE NUMBER OF HOUSEHOLD CLASSES
    ND   – THE NUMBER OF DWELLING CLASSES
    S   – AN NH*ND MATRIX DESCRIBING THE INITIAL ALLOCATION OF
            HOUSEHOLDS TO DWELLINGS
    V   – AN ARRAY OF LENGTH ND, THE NUMBER OF VACANT
            DWELLINGS IN EACH CLASS
    M   – AN NH*ND MATRIX DEFINING THE PROPORTION OF
            HOUSEHOLDS IN EACH "HOUSING SITUATION" WHO WOULD
            LIKE TO MOVE
    Q   – AN NH*ND MATRIX DEFINING THE PROPORTION OF
            HOUSEHOLDS IN EACH "HOUSING SITUATION" WHO ARE
            FINANCIALLY ABLE TO GAIN ACCESS TO 'ANY' OTHER CLASS
            OF DWELLING (EGRESS CONSTRAINT)
    G   – AN NH*ND MATRIX DEFINING THE PROPORTION OF
            HOUSEHOLDS OF EACH HOUSEHOLD CLASS WHO ARE
            FINANCIALLY ABLE TO GAIN ACCESS TO A PARTICULAR
            DWELLING CLASS (ACCESS CONSTRAINT)

THIS DATA IS USED TO CALCULATE THE NUMBER OF HOUSEHOLDS IN
EACH "HOUSING SITUATION" WHO ARE ABLE TO MOVE TO EACH
DWELLING CLASS – THIS "ACTUAL MOVEMENT MATRIX", ER(I,J,L), IS
CALCULATED IN FLOATING POINT AND CONVERTED TO INTEGER FORM,
E(I,J,L) –. WE NEXT CALCULATE THE EFFECTIVE DEMAND FOR EACH
CLASS OF DWELLINGS – EDEM(L) – AND COMPARE DEMAND WITH
VACANCIES IF DEMAND IS LESS THAN OR EQUAL TO VACANCIES THE
ALLOCATION IS STRAIGHTFORWARD; IF DEMAND IS GREATER THAN
VACANCIES HOUSEHOLDS ARE ALLOCATED ON A PROPORTIONAL BASIS.
VACANCIES ARE UPDATED AT EACH ALLOCATION.
FINALLY THE ALLOCATION IS UPDATED.

THE RESULTS OF EACH ITERATION ARE MONITORED BY SUBROUTINE
MONITR AND RESULTS ARE PRINTED BY SUBROUTINE PRINT

Example of test runs

INPUT DATA (based on GLC Housing Surveys I and II, 1967)

NH — The number of household classes = 5

ND — The number of dwelling classes = 6
   ($H_i D_6$ denotes homeless conditions)

S   — The initial allocation of households to dwellings
   (1000 households and 855 occupied dwellings)

	D_1	D_2	D_3	D_4	D_5	D_6
H_1	40	38	68	22	73	35
H_2	15	17	30	15	33	15
H_3	37	32	50	14	47	25
H_4	7	8	20	16	31	35
H_5	15	23	62	38	104	35

V   — The array of vacant stock [65, 10, 10, 5, 5, 0]

M   — Probability of wishing to move

	D_1	D_2	D_3	D_4	D_5	D_6
H_1	·05	·09	·11	·16	·03	·99
H_2	·11	·06	·07	·16	·03	·99
H_3	·12	·06	·13	·06	·03	·99
H_4	·34	·16	·26	·16	·03	·99
H_5	·19	·06	·24	·02	·03	·99

Q   — Egress constraint

	D_1	D_2	D_3	D_4	D_5	D_6
H_1	·01	·60	·20	·11	·18	·95
H_2	·01	·10	·01	·11	·15	·99
H_3	·01	·60	·20	·11	·15	·95
H_4	·02	·90	·30	·14	·18	·99
H_5	·02	·85	·30	·14	·20	·99

G   — Access constraint

	D_1	D_2	D_3	D_4	D_5	D_6
H_1	·20	·90	·25	·20	·50	·99
H_2	·02	·20	·10	·20	·40	·99
H_3	·10	·80	·30	·20	·80	·99
H_4	·20	·95	·60	·30	·80	·99
H_5	·20	·90	·60	·30	·90	·99

Test run with allocation procedure B

		D_1	D_2	D_3	D_4	D_5	D_6
T_0	H_1	40	38	68	22	73	35
	H_2	15	17	30	15	33	15
	H_3	37	32	50	14	47	25
	H_4	7	8	20	16	31	35
	H_5	15	23	62	38	104	35

TOTAL HOMELESS 145 – TOTAL VACANCIES 95

		D_1	D_2	D_3	D_4	D_5	D_6
T_1	H_1	47	40	70	23	74	22
	H_2	15	17	30	15	33	15
	H_3	39	34	51	15	48	18
	H_4	14	32	23	17	11	20
	H_5	23	26	64	39	106	19

TOTAL HOMELESS 94 – TOTAL VACANCIES 44
WISHING TO MOVE/ABLE TO   109
WISHING TO MOVE/UNABLE TO   68
NOT WISHING TO MOVE/ABLE TO   177
NOT WISHING TO MOVE/UNABLE TO   643

		D_1	D_2	D_3	D_4	D_5	D_6
T_2	H_1	51	40	70	23	74	18
	H_2	15	17	30	15	33	15
	H_3	41	34	51	15	48	16
	H_4	18	11	24	17	32	15
	H_5	28	26	64	39	106	14

TOTAL HOMELESS 78 – TOTAL VACANCIES 28
WISHING TO MOVE/ABLE TO   93
WISHING TO MOVE/UNABLE TO   77
NOT WISHING TO MOVE/ABLE TO   175
NOT WISHING TO MOVE/UNABLE TO   656

		D_1	D_2	D_3	D_4	D_5	D_6
T_3	H_1	54	40	70	23	74	15
	H_2	15	17	30	15	33	15
	H_3	43	34	51	15	48	14
	H_4	21	11	24	17	32	12
	H_5	32	26	63	39	106	11

TOTAL HOMELESS 67 – TOTAL VACANCIES 17
WISHING TO MOVE/ABLE TO   82
WISHING TO MOVE/UNABLE TO   73
NOT WISHING TO MOVE/ABLE TO   178
NOT WISHING TO MOVE/UNABLE TO   665

		D_1	D_2	D_3	D_4	D_5	D_6
T_4	H_1	57	40	70	23	74	12
	H_2	15	17	30	15	33	15
	H_3	44	34	51	15	48	13
	H_4	23	11	25	17	32	9
	H_5	35	26	63	39	106	8

TOTAL HOMELESS 57 – TOTAL VACANCIES   7
WISHING TO MOVE/ABLE TO   72
WISHING TO MOVE/UNABLE TO   76
NOT WISHING TO MOVE/ABLE TO   179
NOT WISHING TO MOVE/UNABLE TO   674

		D_1	D_2	D_3	D_4	D_5	D_6
T_5	H_1	58	40	70	23	74	11
	H_2	15	17	30	15	33	15
	H_3	45	34	51	15	48	12
	H_4	24	11	25	17	32	8
	H_5	37	26	62	39	106	7

TOTAL HOMELESS 53 – TOTAL VACANCIES   3
WISHING TO MOVE/ABLE TO   67
WISHING TO MOVE/UNABLE TO   75
NOT WISHING TO MOVE/ABLE TO   179
NOT WISHING TO MOVE/UNABLE TO   679

NO CHANGE IN SUBSEQUENT ITERATIONS

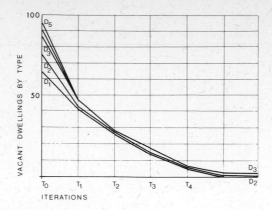

Figure A1   Vacant dwellings

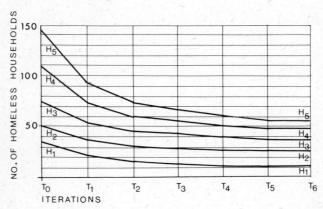

Figure A2   Homeless households

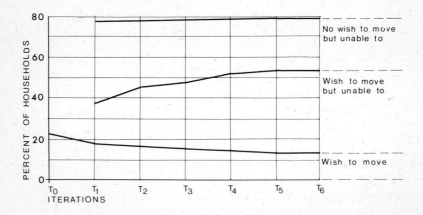

Figure A3   Relationship between the 'wish' and 'ability' to move

188

Appendix B Data sources

Greater London area

This data base consists of two surveys, the GLC Housing Surveys I and II. The first is a 4 per cent sample of housing stock in the Greater London area in 1967. The sample was comprised of every twenty-fifth residential unit then on the Borough Rating Lists. The final sample was 96,229 dwelling units, with a 100 per cent response to the external survey. Some 84 per cent of privately owned dwelling units and 37 per cent of local authority dwellings were internally surveyed. Housing Survey II was for a 9000 sample of Greater London households in 1967. Thirty clusters were created, based on the GLC Index of Housing Stress, and 300 households from each cluster were interviewed. The response rate was 73 per cent leaving a final sample of 6612. Each household selected had been interviewed previously in connection with the condition survey. The GLC have summarised their analyses of the results of these two surveys in the following reports: *The Condition of London's Housing – A Survey* and *The Characteristics of London's Households.*

West Midlands conurbation

The Department of the Environment carried out a housing survey in the West Midlands Conurbation in 1966. The original sample was 3440, selected at random from a revised list of the 1961 Census Conurbation Record Books. With a high response of 88 per cent the final sample was 3005 households. Ruth C. Welch of the Centre for Urban and Regional Studies at the University of Birmingham, prepared a report on this survey entitled *West Midlands Conurbation Housing Survey 1966* .

South Hampshire

This data base also includes two surveys. The first, a condition survey sponsored by the South Hampshire Plan Technical Unit in 1970 comprised a sample of 4680 dwellings. There was a 100 per cent response to the external examination, internal access was achieved in 70 per cent of the sample, and the self-completed questionnaire on income was completed by 70 per cent. The final report on the survey is still not published although results have been used in sections of the *South Hampshire Plan: 1972*. Southampton University sponsored a housing demand study in 1970, which sampled 1000 households and their dwelling units on questions of house condition, housing needs and social mobility. The response rate was 79 per cent of the sample, or a final sample of 740 households. The Department of Sociology and Social Administration at the University prepared a report of their findings in 1972.

Index

Some references are to footnote indices. Where the reader is unable to find the subject on a given page number, he should turn to the notes at the end of the chapter for a lead.

The authors

Bev Nutt gained a degree in Architecture at University College London in 1963. Following a period in architectural practice he has been Deputy Director of the Joint Unit for Planning Research since 1969 and was appointed Senior Lecturer at the School of Environmental Studies, University College London, in 1975.

Bruce Walker has a degree in Economics and has since undertaken research at the University of Kent and in the Joint Unit for Planning Research. He is now Lecturer in Economic Aspects of Urban Studies, Urban and Regional Planning, at Lanchester Polytechnic.

Susan Holliday gained her BA at Goucher College, Towson, USA and then became a Research Assistant in the Joint Unit for Planning Research. She is now engaged in postgraduate studies in Town Planning at University College London.

Dan Sears studied Architecture at University College London and, after a period in architectural practice, he was attached to the Operational Research Unit at the Department of Health and Social Security. Since 1970 he has been a research associate in the Joint Unit for Planning Research.